Starting and Running a Nonprofit Organization

Starting
and Running
a Nonprofit
Organization

Joan M. Hummel

UNIVERSITY OF MINNESOTA PRESS □ MINNEAPOLIS

Published by the University of Minnesota Press,
2037 University Avenue Southeast,
Minneapolis, Minnesota 55414

Library of Congress Cataloging in Publication Data

Hummel, Joan M
    Starting and running a nonprofit organization.
    Bibliography: p.
    Includes index.
    1. Corporations, Nonprofit—Management. I. Title.
HD38.H84   658'.048   80-15210
ISBN 0-8166-0986-1
ISBN 0-8166-0989-6 (pbk.)

Thanks...

To those who contributed to *Starting and Running a Nonprofit Organization*:

    Douglas Johnson
    David Nelson
    Albert Veranth

To those who reviewed chapters of *Starting and Running a Nonprofit Organization*:

    Terri Barreiro, Dayton-Hudson Foundation
    Andrew Boss, St. Anthony Park State Bank
    Jerry Catt, Jerry V. Catt and Associates
    Audrey Cenedella, Medtronic, Inc.
    Jane Cooper, Padilla and Speer, Inc.
    Ginny Greenman, Control Data, Inc.
    Richard Mammen, Katahdin: A Workshop for Youth
    Jackie Reis, Minnesota Council on Foundations
    Bodo Suemnig, Washington County Community Corrections
    Galen Wells, attorney, Hoerner Waldorf Champion
        International Corporation
    The staff of Enablers

To those who helped fund the development of the handbook:

    Pillsbury Company Foundation
    The Honeywell Fund

Enablers...

Enablers is a nonprofit organization dedicated to the improvement of services offered to youth in the Minneapolis-St. Paul area. It has provided informational services and technical assistance to youth service organizations, community planners, and other groups and individuals.

For ten years, Enablers provided assistance to hot-lines, community clinics, drug treatment centers, alternative schools, group homes, drop-in centers, delinquency intervention programs, and recreational programs throughout the Twin Cities area. Many of the groups served were in the fledgling or regrouping stage of development. In order to meet their needs, consulting and training workshops have been provided by Enablers in most of the areas covered by this handbook.

About *Starting and Running a Nonprofit Organization...*

This handbook is designed for those who are forming new programs or reorganizing existing agencies. It provides how-to information for putting together a small, nonprofit organization. It is hoped that *Nonprofit Organizations* will be useful to planning groups, community organizers, agency directors, boards of directors, and coordinating groups working on various issues and in different service areas.

Samples, worksheets, and bibliographies have been included to make this guide applicable to individual organizations. The handbook has been designed so that the worksheets can be duplicated and used easily. Although the material is copyrighted, permission for duplication of the worksheets is granted, providing that Enablers and *Starting and Running a Nonprofit Organization* are credited as the source.

Although some of the information about the laws affecting nonprofit organizations applies specifically to Minnesota, the handbook can be used by program planners as a tool to research the state laws that apply to nonprofit organizations in any state.

In addition to the bibliographies at the ends of some of the chapters, there is a bibliography on nonprofit management at the end of the text. It describes resources that discuss the ongoing managment concerns of nonprofit organizations.

Contents

Starting and Running a Nonprofit Organization

Introduction

The French politician Alexis de Tocqueville wrote about 150 years ago that "Americans are forever forming associations." Today, a great many services are provided to the American public by nonprofit associations, in addition to the services provided by state and national governments and "for profit" businesses and corporations. The United States' tradition of supporting an extensive nonprofit sector is a strong one.

Throughout the country, nonprofit organizations work with children, young people, and the elderly, the mentally and physically handicapped, and the underprivileged. They promote the arts. They protect and promote the rights of special interest groups, such as consumers and environmentalists. They foster the development of professionals in a variety of fields. They provide recreational and educational opportunities. Yet, in spite of their varying goals and directions, all nonprofit organizations stand on a common ground. They are groups of people getting together around a mutual interest in order to perform a community service. The number of such groups in the United States has mushroomed to an estimated six million. The largest of these groups are, of course, well known; examples include the Girl Scouts, the Jaycees, the PTA, the American Medical Association, and the Sierra Club. And, in every city and town, there are hospitals, colleges, museums, symphonies, and chambers of commerce.

There is also a new wave of grassroots organizations, young, struggling groups put together by members of a community who have an issue on their minds and who, most often, have little or no experience in agency development and very little money in their pockets. Local chapters of the Grey Panthers are being organized by senior citizens to protect their rights. Neighborhood residents are organizing around housing issues. Parents who fear they may abuse their children are putting together chapters of Parents

Anonymous. Citizens who are concerned about the environmental impact of impending projects are organizing to work against them. In the light of dwindling natural resources, groups have developed to promote the use of alternative sources of energy and energy conservation. In many communities, women's groups have opened homes, or "shelters," for battered women. The range of concerns of this new wave of nonprofits is enormous.

Organizations develop from a seed—a common concern, a critical issue, a central purpose. This focus becomes the organization's mission. Individuals and groups who find they have a common concern and want to do something about it begin talking, meeting, and planning their directions. One direction such a group might take is forming an organization—with a separate name, identity, purpose, and possibly a staff or membership. The most common form an organization of this nature can take is that of a nonprofit corporation. (The benefits derived from this form of organization are discussed in the chapter on legal aspects.)

What are the other directions that could be considered? There may be means of achieving goals other than by forming an organization. If a group does not need to raise much money to achieve its purpose, it may be able to function on a less formal basis. The group may be able to accomplish its goal by acting as a loosely knit committee. If the group is uncertain about the need to form a permanent, ongoing organization, it might find an established organization sympathetic to its "cause" that would act as a "foster parent" on a temporary basis. It might provide office space and a telephone and serve as a fiscal agent for any money the group raises; the group would fall under the umbrella of the parent agency. If a group were concerned that a certain type of service be made available to a community, it could work with an existing organization in the same service area to develop the specific type of program needed. Or the group could find that a neighboring community has the type of organization it wanted, and it could try to persuade the organization to open a branch in its community.

After considering these options, a group may still decide that it wants to establish a separate, legal identity to accomplish its mission. It may form a nonprofit corporation whether or not it has a paid staff or a separate office, offers established programs to the general public, or solicits fees from its participants.

Many nonprofits function as all-volunteer associations, with no paid staff. Some are designed this way on an ongoing basis. Many groups with paying members function this way. Others begin as volunteer organizations with plans to add paid staff as they expand. Many others, especially direct service agencies, need a paid staff in order to operate. When considering these alternative formats, a group should keep in mind that the form it has decided is most feasible for the organization in its infancy does not have to be permanent. Organizations can change and grow and develop different ways of functioning as they become necessary.

A group needs more than an issue, a goal, or a mission in order to make something happen. It needs a well-thought-out program, a sound financial base, an effective staff and board of directors, and good community relations. These are areas of management expertise that can be developed by grassroots organizers with time and effort.

In order to provide assistance to a greater number of small, nonprofit agencies in their early or developing stages, Enablers has compiled this handbook, which will serve as an introduction to the basic concepts and skills of agency planning and development. Since nonprofit organizations must rely on limited resources, it is imperative that they learn to develop their human and monetary assets to the fullest. Many worthwhile and needed programs ultimately fail to reach their goals because they were not put together well; their organizational skeletons were too weak to carry the weight. In the end, it is the client and the community who are affected most by such a failure. The tradition of community service will be carried on by the newest crop of nonprofits if the roots they plant in their early stages are strong ones.

A Checklist of Things
to Be Done When Starting
a Nonprofit Organization

Projected Date of Completion	*Completion Checkoff*	
————	————	*Determine purpose and structure.* Hold initial planning (possibly informal) meeting(s) to establish consensus on the purposes and the form of the proposed organization. Delegate responsibilities for drafting bylaws, filing for incorporation, developing a program plan and budget, and planning for fund raising.
————	————	*Form initial board of directors.* A formal board of directors is required for incorporation and is desired by those considering initial funding proposals.
————	————	*File articles of incorporation.* Most funding sources deal only with organizations incorporated as nonprofits.
————	————	*Draft bylaws.* Since these make up the "rule-book" for running an organization, it is helpful to draft them during the early stages of development. In addition, bylaws must accompany the application for tax exemption.

6

Projected Date of Completion	*Completion Checkoff*	
_____	_____	*Determine program plan.* Develop written goals and objectives, a work plan, and a service description for at least a one-year period.
_____	_____	*Develop a budget.* Anticipate expenditures and income for the first full year.
_____	_____	*Draft a fund-raising plan.* Determine appropriate sources from which to seek funding, outline approach to fundors, and project a fund-raising timetable.
_____	_____	*Hold formal organizational meeting.* At an official meeting of the board of directors, accept the articles of incorporation, adopt the bylaws, elect officers, authorize tax-exemption application, authorize any financial transactions, and continue program planning.
_____	_____	*Establish a recordkeeping system.* The recordkeeping system will be used for preserving corporate documents, reports, and all minutes of the board meetings. These are the official records of the organization and must be maintained for the life of the corporation.
_____	_____	*File 1023 application with the Internal Revenue Service to obtain 501(c)(3) tax exemption from corporate income taxes.* This frees donors from paying taxes on funds donated to the organization and, in essence, makes it "fundable."
_____	_____	*File charitable trust registration with the state.*

Projected Date of Completion	*Completion Checkoff*	
_____	_____	*Apply for solicitation license from local municipality.* Check with local officials of the cities in which the organization will be raising funds to determine whether a license is necessary.
_____	_____	*Establish a bookkeeping/accounting system.* Only a simple system will be needed until the organization begins to receive major grants and to conduct program activities. However, anticipate the organization's financial record-keeping needs for these later stages of development and develop an accounting system that can meet these needs.
_____	_____	*Develop and submit fund-raising proposals.* Government grants may be solicited when incorporation has been established. Solicitation of private foundation grants will not be very successful before the Internal Revenue Service formally recognizes the organization's 501(c)(3) tax exemption by sending out a letter.
_____	_____	*File employer registration with federal and state government agencies for income tax withholding.* The organization will receive a federal employer number.
_____	_____	*Decide about Social Security contributions.* If the decision is yes, notify the Social Security office, since all 501(c)(3) organizations are automatically exempt.
_____	_____	*File for state income tax exemption upon receipt of federal exemption.*

Projected Date of Completion	*Completion Checkoff*	
_____	_____	*Apply for state sales tax exemption.* The organization will receive a certificate of exempt status with its sales-tax exemption number.
_____	_____	*Register with state unemployment insurance program.* This is done through the state department of employment after the organization begins operating.
_____	_____	*Apply for property tax exemption, if appropriate,* with local tax assessor's office.
_____	_____	*Obtain liability insurance.* Such insurance covers the organization's property and insures the organization against personal injury suits by clients and guests.
_____	_____	*Apply for nonprofit bulk mail permit from post office.* Such a permit is beneficial if the organization plans mailings of over 200 pieces of material.
_____	_____	*Develop personnel policies.* This should be done within the first year of operation.
_____	_____	*Begin program activities.* Staff may be hired, space rented, and program activities started any time, depending on the solidification of program plans and of a significant portion of the proposed funding. The board of directors must determine when the program should actually begin functioning.

Note: This checklist was prepared as a guide for persons who are considering forming a nonprofit organization. Depending on the type of program and the sources of funding, further registration, reporting, or licensing may be required.

Boards of Directors: "Behind Every Good Organization..."

Your program owes its existence to a creative spark that went off in the heads of a few concerned individuals who came up with a good idea—the original organizers of your program. Your organization will keep going, however, because this idea was nurtured and given the opportunity to develop, change, and expand by another group of people—the board of directors.

This group is not static; it develops as the organization itself develops. The board's size, structure, and composition should respond to the changing needs of your organization. In the beginning, the initial organizers of a program seek out other people with the interest and skill necessary to translate their ideas into a functioning service. When the organization incorporates, this group serves officially as the initial board of directors. As the organization develops, the membership of the board will change. In spite of the inevitable turnover in the board's membership, the corporate body of the board will provide continuity for the nonprofit corporation.

The board of directors is a group legally, financially, and morally responsible for the total operation and conduct of the nonprofit corporation. It is its job to see that the organization is carrying out its mission in a manner that is ethical, effective, and fiscally accountable.

Volunteer boards of directors are the trustees of the nonprofit corporation and are answerable to the agency's financial contributors, the recipients of its services, and the government units that monitor nonprofit corporations. Individual board members must be conscious of the responsibility they undertake in the name of the corporation.

WHAT DOES THE BOARD OF DIRECTORS DO?

The board of directors provides the continuity on which your organization is based. Individual members of the staff and the board come and go, but the entity of the board exists as long as your organization does. Individual members of the board together form a corporate body that has the overall responsibility for your organization.

What are the specific functions of the board of directors? Board members generally assume responsibilities in the following areas.

Budget and Finance

The board members approve the budget, which is generally prepared by the executive director of the agency. They monitor program expenditures and determine sound fiscal policy and internal control practices. They assume responsibility for the fiscal accountability of the organization. (These finance-related functions are probably the ones most important to the board.)

Planning

Members of the board of directors approve the long-range plans of the organization, including the program's goals and objectives. They assist the staff in the development of these plans and set organizational priorities for action.

Fund Raising

Board members ensure that adequate funds are available for financing the agency's operations. They approve the general fund-raising methods used by the organization. They participate in fund-raising activities, and individual board members may serve as the agency's contact with specific sources of funds.

Policy

Members of the board determine the organization's policies. *Policies* can be defined as the broad guidelines that provide a framework for future decision making. Policies are reflected in procedures, which are the more specific, narrow parameters that are used in organizational decision making.

Procedures clarify what steps must be taken, what rules must be followed, and who must be included in the process. Procedures are generally formulated by the staff rather than by the board.

Personnel

The board of directors hires the executive director, monitors the effectiveness of the director's performance, and removes the director when his or her performance is unsatisfactory. It determines the salary scales and benefits for the staff, and it develops personnel policies. (However, staff members are hired, evaluated, and, if necessary, removed by the executive director, not the board.)

Public Relations

The board of directors communicates with fundors, community leaders, and other interested parties about the program. It represents the agency in the community. And it advises the staff in development of public relations plans.

Program Evaluation

Board members monitor the program's effectiveness. They review program-evaluation procedures on a regular basis, and they advise the staff on the agency's self-evaluation.

Board Development

The board of directors determines the structure of the board and committee membership. It nominates and selects new board members and sets the standards for its own periodic self-evaluation. (This self-evaluation process is rare among nonprofit boards, but it can be an important means of maintaining an effective and qualified board of directors.)

Advising

The board offers administrative guidance to the executive director and advises the staff in the various program areas. Small agencies with a limited staff often use the expertise of board members, who give advice or provide a new perspective on problems.

GETTING ORGANIZED

How are the functions of the board of directors carried out? The board of directors must organize itself in a manner that allows its duties to be carried out quickly and responsibly.

Board structure, of course, varies. The bylaws of your organization are the general rules that govern the organization and define the board's composition and structure. These rules should allow the board to be flexible enough to respond to the changing needs of the organization.

Officers

The board selects one of its members to be president. The president presides at meetings, keeps the group directed toward its goals, delegates responsibility for tasks to other members or committees, and serves as the primary contact between the board and the executive director and other staff members. The president is responsible for keeping the group—the directors—functioning effectively.

Other officers who are designated by most boards of directors include the vice-president, secretary, and treasurer, as outlined in the organization's bylaws. The vice-president acts in place of the president in the latter's absence. The treasurer has general responsibility for the agency's funds and accounts. The secretary is responsible for the written records of the board of directors, including the minutes of the meetings. (The secretary's responsibilities are sometimes delegated to a staff member.)

Committees

Dividing work by committees is the most effective means of operation for some organizations. If your board is small enough, it can usually deal as a body with the business of the corporation, with no need for committee work. But, if your board is fairly large, it may choose to divide its main concerns among standing committees, which report to the board as a whole.

Even if your organization does not choose to develop an extensive committee structure, it may have an *executive committee* composed of the officers of the corporation and the chairs of any other committees. Executive committees fulfill a variety of roles. They are usually given decision-making authority for urgent business during the periods between board meetings. An executive committee can serve as a special advisory group to the executive director, and it can be responsible for planning other board activities and determining the agendas of board meetings.

Standing (or ongoing) committees generally correspond to the various areas of the board's responsibility. Board members with interest and expertise in specific areas are appointed, generally by the board's president, to serve on standing committees.

Your organization must determine its committee structure carefully, keeping in mind the size of the board, the amount of time the board members have available, and the needs of the organization. A relatively young agency may have a very limited committee structure, but it may add more committees as it develops. If organizations do not divide into working committees, the tasks performed by such committees must be handled by the board as a whole.

Common types of standing committees include finance, personnel, nominating, public relations, and program committees. Your board of directors may include any number of these or none of them. Another option is having the executive committee take on the tasks of one or more of these types of subcommittees.

The *finance committee* monitors fiscal operations, assists the director in developing an annual budget, develops a fund-raising plan, and helps carry out this plan.

The *nominating committee* recommends individuals to serve as board members and officers, recommends the criteria for selection of new board members, provides orientation to new members, and reviews the participation of current members.

The *personnel committee* reviews personnel needs, determines salaries and benefits, develops personnel policies, and provides for grievance procedures.

The *public relations committee* disseminates information about the organization to the agency's different publics through the media and/or personal presentations.

Program committees advise the staff in program areas, recommend service policies, monitor the agency's services, and provide the board with detailed information regarding these services.

As an alternative (or addition) to standing committees, many boards utilize "ad hoc" committees—those formed to do one job and then disband when the task has been completed. For instance, a special committee may be formed in the absence of a personnel committee to search for a new executive director and disband after the position has been filled. Or an ad hoc committee could be formed to advise the staff on a specific, short-term project.

Communication

Regular channels of communication must be set up among board members and between the board and the staff. The most common of these communication channels are periodic board meetings. Boards of directors of nonprofit corporations are generally required by state law to have at least one board meeting each year. Small, active boards tend to have monthly meetings. Larger boards may meet only quarterly to deal with major issues while smaller committees of board members work on other organizational concerns between the quarterly board meetings. Generally, board meetings should be held at least four times a year. Your organization must determine a meeting schedule that meets its needs and operates within the time constraints of its board members.

The minutes of board meetings are very important for your organization. They are the only legal records of a nonprofit corporation. All controversial or potentially controversial issues (such as personnel grievances, client-policy issues, and legal questions) or those involving substantial amounts of money should be raised at meetings of the board, with records of the discussions held and the decisions made included in the minutes. The minutes of executive committee meetings should also be recorded. Information included in these minutes can protect the corporation if legal action were ever taken against it.

In addition to calling board and committee meetings, the president of your board should meet regularly with the executive director and with other key board members, such as officers and committee chairs. There should be sufficient opportunity for the exchange of staff opinions and recommendations with the board and for board opinions and decisions with the staff.

The executive director plays a major role in keeping communication channels open and vital. The director should ensure that (1) board members clearly understand the goals of the agency and their role in the organization; (2) scheduled meetings are necessary and deal with important issues; (3) specific agendas and meeting notices are sent well in advance of meetings and accurate minutes are sent soon after the meetings take place; and (4) staff and board members interact.

WHO'S ON THE BOARD?

How Many Members Should a Board Include?

State law determines the minimum size of the board of a nonprofit corporation. By law, boards of nonprofit corporations in Minnesota are required to have at least three members. Organizations in different states should check with their secretary of state regarding the size requirements for boards of directors. The ideal size of the board depends on the needs of your organization. The board should be large enough to obtain broad-based community support and input and yet small enough to be efficient. Most boards have between twelve and thirty members. In general, the size and diversity of an organization is reflected in the size of its board.

Who Should Be on the Board?

Ideally, the composition of the board should be varied enough to provide variety in areas of expertise and perspective. Board members should be selected according to what they can provide your organization, especially in the following areas.

Competence in Administrative Areas: The board should include members experienced in finance and accounting, agency management, law, public relations, and fund raising.

Competence in Program Areas: The purpose of your organization and the services it offers should be considered in the selection of board members. For instance, the board of a health clinic for teenagers should probably include medical personnel and others with a background in adolescent health needs and practices. An environmental group may want to include a scientist with relevant expertise as a board member.

Bridge to Constituencies: Members of the target population of the program and representatives of other related agencies should be included on the board. For instance, the board of a day-care center should include some parents. The board of a delinquency-prevention program should probably include a teacher, a police officer, a juvenile-court representative, and some youths.

Community Leadership: Some members of the board should have influence in the community, access to resources, and/or affiliations with other organizations of importance to your own.

Other Factors: In order to increase the representativeness of the board, members may be selected in part to provide balance in the areas of age, sex, ethnic background, geographic alignment, et cetera.

Some organizations develop selection criteria for board members that are based on percentages or numbers of members from different categories like those described above. This practice can help assure that board membership includes a diverse representation of backgrounds, skills, and viewpoints. Refer to the board composition chart at the end of this chapter to analyze or plan the makeup of your own board of directors.

What Should You Look for in a Board Member?

Board members should be selected for the skills and resources that they can contribute to your organization. If current or potential board members do not fit into any of the categories outlined, they should be analyzed in terms of their special strengths or skills. If these are found wanting, such individuals may not be effective members of your organization's board of directors.

Another major factor to consider is the amount of time and energy a potential member may be able to commit to your organization. Try to evaluate the time required of your board members and discuss your needs with the potential members. If their ability to participate is extremely limited, you may wish to find others who can make a stronger commitment.

Perhaps the most important qualifications for board membership are an interest in the work of the organization, a commitment to its goals, the ability to work as a team member, and a willingness to ask questions, offer criticism, and make suggestions.

How Do You Invite Someone to Join Your Board?

Your initial contact with potential board members is an important one. You want them to know what is exciting and interesting about your organization. You want to tell them that being on your board of directors is worthwhile. On the other hand, you want to tell them directly how much time and what skills you need from them. If there is someone on your board who knows the member you are considering, this board member is the best contact with the potential member. Otherwise, another board member should be assigned to interview each potential member.

Personal meetings should be arranged between a current board member and a potential member, possibly over lunch or in another social situation. There should be enough time for detailed discussion about your organization and the role of your board members in it. Prospective members should not be rushed for an answer. You should encourage them to take some time to consider joining your board. New board members who are well informed about the organization, including its problems, and about their expected role are more likely to be participating and effective members.

GETTING ORIENTED

When discussing board involvement with potential members, you should speak clearly about why they were selected; what capacity they will serve; what skills, and viewpoints, you want them to contribute; the amount of time they will be expected to contribute for meetings and other activities; the length of their terms on the board; the committee work they will be expected to do; and the possible costs to them as members: lunches, travel, time away from work, et cetera. In exchange, ask prospective board members what they want to contribute to your organization and how their participation can be easily and best utilized by your organization. Remember that board members need rewards, too, and consider what your organization can give to its board members: the satisfaction of serving the community, social contacts, and experience in policy making, fund raising, or other aspects of agency administration.

In order for board members to function effectively, they must first have a thorough understanding of the organization they serve. New members, as individuals or as a group, should be introduced to the program by current board or staff members. This introduction should include information about the history of the program and the services provided; a discussion of the goals and the philosophy of the organization; a review of the minutes of recent board meetings; and a tour of the program's facility and an introduction to all the staff members, when that is feasible. Each board member should receive a written manual that includes information on the goals and objectives for the current year; a copy of the budget and a list of funding sources; the bylaws of the corporation; an organizational chart outlining lines of authority and communication; copies of recent proposals, reports, and brochures; the names, addresses, and phone numbers of the board and the staff; and a list of current committee assignments.

In order to have a representative board, your organization may recruit board members with little or no background in program management or board processes. Representatives of the client group are especially likely to lack this expertise. In such cases, special training should be provided so that these members may contribute fully. Areas of training for these members should include group-process skills, Robert's Rules of Order, reading and understanding a budget, and the legal requirements for nonprofit corporations.

Orientation programs for new board members and annual board/staff retreats are both good means for informing board members about the organization's activities.

Effective boards of directors are not developed overnight. Instead, they must be carefully nurtured and maintained. But the contributions that a committed and skilled board bring to your organization are well worth the hard work, the conflicts, the periodic tedium, and the frustration that are common even among the most "together" of boards.

BOARD COMPOSITION CHART

Management Expertise	Public Relations																													
	Marketing																													
	Personnel																													
	Training/Development																													
	Accounting																													
	Fiscal Planning																													
	Fund Raising																													
	Law																													
	Board Leadership																													
Program Expertise	Other																													
	Private Practice																													
	Media																													
	Religious																													
	Political																													
	Educational																													
	Cultural																													
	Governmental																													
	Corporate																													
	Social Service Agency																													
Sector	Community/Client Representative																													
	Community Organization																													
	Vocational																													
	Health/Welfare																													
	Cultural/Arts																													
	Education/Research																													
	Corrections/Justice																													
	Recreation																													
	Counseling																													
Residence	Northwest																													
	Southwest																													
	Northeast																													
	Southeast																													
	Central																													
Ethnic Background	Asian																													
	Native American																													
	Hispanic																													
	Black																													
	White																													
Sex	Female																													
	Male																													
Age	Over 65																													
	46–65																													
	30–45																													
	20–29																													
	13–19																													
BOARD MEMBERS																														

Bibliography

The Effective Board. By Cyril O. Houle. New York: Association Press, 1960. An excellent resource for new and experienced board members. Explains the types of boards and examines the roles and needs of individual board members, board structure, board-staff relations, and ways of improving board operation. (174 pages)

The Effective Director in Action. By K. Louden and J. Zusman. New York: AMACOM (a division of the American Management Association), 1975. Covers the roles and responsibilities of corporate board members, including corporate accountability, fiscal and organizational planning, and standards of performance. Also discusses the role of public agency boards in government and the nonprofit sector and their special problems and responsibilities. (190 pages)

The Effective Voluntary Board of Directors: What It Is and How It Works. By William Conrad and William Glenn. Chicago: Swallow Press, 1975. Written for the board members and professional staff of nonprofit organizations. Discusses board organization, board-staff relations, the role and function of committees, policy making, board meetings, membership and the different kinds of boards. (185 pages)

Guide for Board Organization in Social Agencies. Child Welfare League of America, 67 Irving Place, New York, N.Y. 10003, 1975. Good, basic orientation for boards and staff. Topics include board organizations, bylaws, committees, the role of the executive director, agency evaluation, fiscal accountability, and board manuals. (36 pages)

The Volunteer Board Member in Philanthropy. National Information Bureau, 419 Park Avenue, New York, N.Y. 10016, 1975. Directed toward board members. Discusses the role of boards, the impact of board failures, myths about boards, and a checklist for rating the performance of individual members and the board as a group. (23 pages)

Bylaws:
Playing by the Rules

Bylaws are the rulebook for a nonprofit corporation. They govern the internal affairs of your organization. They determine who has power and how that power will work. They give structure to your organization, help prevent conflicts and disagreements, and protect against the misuse of funds. Bylaws are required by the Internal Revenue Service for tax exemption and are provided for by state law.

Primarily, bylaws outline how your board of directors will operate, and they specify the size of the board, the selection and tenure of board members, the number of board meetings, the number of officers and committees, the financial and legal procedures, and the purpose of the organization.

Bylaws should be tailored to meet the needs of your organization. It can be very helpful to review bylaws of similar organizations during the development of your own, but don't simply adopt a set of bylaws formulated by someone else. Decide how you want your own organization to function. Program organizers should discuss and determine how they wish to operate. Remember that these rules may not be appropriate forever; your bylaws should outline steps by which they can be revised when it becomes necessary or desirable.

Although bylaws should be specific enough to be useful guidelines, they should also be flexible. Allow some room for the changing needs of your organization. For instance, it may be helpful to specify a range for the number of directors rather than a specific number.

The following questionnaire and list of sample bylaws outline the concerns that bylaws should address. After decisions in these areas have been made by the board of directors, they should be written as formal bylaws. You should have these reviewed by an attorney to ensure that they meet legal requirements. If each of the questions in the following outline have been answered, your bylaws should be acceptable. Although the law does not require that you address all of the following items, it is strongly recommended, and expected, that the bylaws of nonprofit corporations include all of this information.

Bylaws should be formally adopted during the first official meeting of the board of directors following incorporation. The bylaws must be included with your application for federal tax exemption from the Internal Revenue Service.

BYLAWS GUIDE:
OUTLINE OF DECISIONS TO BE MADE
REGARDING ORGANIZATION STRUCTURE AND FUNCTION

I. What is the PURPOSE of the organization?

II. Where will the organization be LOCATED?

III. Will the organization have MEMBERS?

There is a distinction between members of an organization and members of its board of directors. The membership of a corporation includes a large group of people who meet only once or a few times a year. Members usually elect the board of directors and adopt or revise bylaws, and they may have additional powers. Membership gives an organization much broader community representation. Some types of organizations, such as day-care centers and community action groups, are more likely to have members than others.

If the organization does not have a separate membership, bylaws should indicate that members of the corporation will consist only of the members of the board of directors. If there is a separate membership, the following questions should be addressed.

1. What are the QUALIFICATIONS for membership?

2. How are members SELECTED?

3. What is the LENGTH of membership? The areas of termination, resignation, reinstatement, and transfer of membership should also be considered.

4. POWERS: What can be decided at meetings of members?

5. What is the least number of times the members should hold a MEETING during a year? (They must meet at least once a year.)

6. QUORUM: How many members must be present for a members' meeting to be able to do official business? (It is not advisable to set a quorum that will be difficult to reach.)

7. Who can CALL a meeting; what are the NOTIFICATION requirements (type of notice, how many days in advance) regarding meetings; who will CHAIR membership meetings?

8. Can members vote by PROXY? How many VOTES of those present are needed to pass a motion at a members' meeting?

IV. What will the structure of the BOARD OF DIRECTORS BE?

The board of directors of a corporation makes most of the decisions about how the organization will operate and selects the executive director of the organization.

1. What will the SIZE of the board of directors be?

   Minnesota law requires that there be at least three members on a board. Although many organizations have either very small or very large boards, between nine and nineteen members seems to be a good size for discussion and decision making.

2. Who is ELIGIBLE to be a member of the board of directors? If there are certain groups who should be represented, these should be indicated.

3. How are the members SELECTED?

4. TENURE: How long do board members serve? May they serve two or more consecutive terms?

   Usually, board members serve one-, two-, or three-year terms. Terms can be "staggered" so that only part of the board is elected each year. Often, the number of terms a member can serve is limited in order to encourage new input. The goal is stability without stagnation.

5. How are board members who resign during their terms REPLACED?

6. Can board members be REMOVED from the board of directors before their terms are over? If so, how? Under what conditions?

7. Will board members be COMPENSATED for time, services, transportation, and other expenses? Generally, bylaws indicate that board members will not be paid for time and services. State laws governing incorporation should be checked to determine whether or not board members can receive monetary compensation.

V. How are the MEETINGS of the board of directors structured?

1. What is the MINIMUM NUMBER of times the board of directors must meet during a one-year period?

   They must meet at least once annually.

2. Who may call a SPECIAL MEETING of the board?

3. What are the NOTIFICATION requirements regarding meetings?

   Bylaws generally indicate that written notice regarding the time and place of regular meetings must be sent to all board members a certain number of days prior to the meeting.

4. What is the QUORUM for a board of directors' meeting?

5. Is a simple MAJORITY (votes of half of the board members present, plus one) sufficient to pass a motion at a meeting of the board?

6. Can board members vote by PROXY?

7. What RULES or procedures will be used to conduct meetings?

   Robert's Rules of Order are commonly used.

VI. What role will OFFICERS have in the organization?

1. What OFFICERS does the corporation have (chairman or president, vice-chairman or vice-president, secretary, treasurer, others)?

2. How are the officers ELECTED?

3. TENURE: How long do the officers serve?

4. How can officers be REMOVED from their positions?

5. How can officers be REPLACED if they resign or are removed before the end of their terms?

6. What are the specific POWERS AND DUTIES of each of the officers?

VII. What will the structure of the COMMITTEES be?

Most boards use committees to some degree. Larger boards, especially, tend to designate work and responsibility to smaller committees. Bylaws can merely mention that committees may be set up and outline how they would work; they can name specific committees and their functions; or they can name only one or two committees and allow for the formation of others.

1. What STANDING COMMITTEES will the board of directors have?

2. What SIZE will these committees be and what will be their DUTIES?

3. May OTHER COMMITTEES be formed for specific purposes?

4. How will committee MEMBERS and chairs be appointed? How long will they serve?

VIII. What SPECIAL RULES will apply to the corporation?

1. Does the corporation have the power to INDEMNIFY (protect from liability) its board members?

2. Will the board members be authorized to execute CONTRACTS on behalf of the organization?

3. How will CHECKS AND DEPOSITS be handled by the corporation?

Who is authorized to sign checks and deposit or withdraw money? Is more than one signature required?

4. Which BOOKS AND RECORDS will be kept and where will they be located?

5. Will there be MEMBERSHIP DUES? How will these be handled?

6. What is the FISCAL YEAR of the corporation?

IX. If the organization DISSOLVES, how will that be done and what will be done with the assets of the corporation?

X. How can the BYLAWS be AMENDED?

MODEL SET OF BYLAWS

These model bylaws are presented only as a guide for the formation of your own bylaws. Although bylaws vary in format, structure, and detail, the bylaws of most organizations include all of the information that this model includes. This is merely a sample. Each organization should develop a set of bylaws suitable to its own purposes, and the effect of each of these "rules" on the function of the organization should be carefully considered during the process of development.

ARTICLE I. PURPOSE

The corporation has been organized to operate exclusively for charitable purposes, including but not limited to:

(1)
    (Outline the purposes of your organization as described in
(2)
    your articles of incorporation)
(3)

ARTICLE II. LOCATION

The principal office of the corporation, at which the general business of the corporation will be transacted and where the records of the corporation will be kept, will be at such place in the metropolitan area, state of Minnesota, as may be fixed from time to time by the board of directors. Unless otherwise fixed, it will be at ___(address)___.

ARTICLE III. MEMBERS

Members of the corporation will consist only of the members of the board of directors.

OR

ARTICLE III. MEMBERS

Section 1. The qualifications for membership will be _____
_____.

Section 2. Persons will be selected for membership by _____
_____.

Section 3. Each member will serve _____(tenure)_____.

Section 4: The duties of the membership of this corporation will include _____ .

Section 5: An annual meeting of the members will be held in _____ _____ of each year. Special meetings of the members may be called _____ (by whom) _____ _____ (and how) _____ .

Section 6: The quorum of a membership meeting will be _____ .

Section 7: Notice of meetings of the membership must be sent to each member and must be mailed or delivered at least _____ days prior to the day such a meeting will be held.

Section 8: Membership meetings will be chaired by _____ .

Section 9: Members __(may/may not)__ vote by proxy at any meeting of members.

ARTICLE IV. BOARD OF DIRECTORS

Section 1: The number of members of the board of directors of this corporation will be not less than _____ or more than _____ .

Section 2: Directors will be representative of _(list groups to be represented)_ in the ___(geographic)___ area and will share the mission and goals of the corporation. This corporation is committed to a policy of fair representation on the board of directors, which does not discriminate on the basis of race, physical handicap, sex, color, religion, sexual orientation, or age.

Section 3. Election of new directors or election of current directors to a second term will occur as the first item of business at the annual meeting of the corporation. Directors will be elected by a majority vote of the current directors.

Section 4. The term of each director of the corporation will be _____ year(s). No director will serve more than _____ consecutive terms.

Section 5: When a director dies, resigns, or is removed, the board may elect a director to serve for the duration of the unexpired term.

Section 6. Any director may be removed from the board of directors by an affirmative vote of the majority of directors present at an official meeting of the board. Notice of the proposed removal will be given to members with the notice of the meeting. The director involved will be given an opportunity to be present and to be heard at the meeting at which his or her removal is considered.

Section 7: No compensation will be paid to any member of the board of directors for services as a member of the board. By resolution of the board, reasonable expenses may be allowed for attendance at regular and special meetings of the board.

ARTICLE V. MEETINGS OF THE BOARD OF DIRECTORS

Section 1. An annual meeting of the board of directors will be held in _____ of each year for the purpose of electing officers and directors. In addition to its annual meeting, the board of directors will hold regular meetings at least _____ times each calendar year at such place as may be designated in the notice of the meeting.

Section 2. Special meetings of the board of directors may be called at any time by the president of the corporation or in his or her absence by the vice-president or upon receipt of a request therefore signed by _____ or more directors or by a majority of the full-time, permanent paid staff of the corporation.

Section 3. Notice of regular, special, and annual meetings will be mailed at least _____ days prior to the day such meeting is to be held. Any director of the corporation may make written waiver of notice before, at, or after a meeting. The waiver will be filed with the person who has been designated to act as secretary of the meeting; this person will enter it in the record of the meeting. Appearance at a meeting is deemed a waiver unless the director attends for the express purpose of asserting the illegality of the meeting.

Section 4: At all meetings of the board of directors, each director present will be entitled to cast one vote on any motion coming before the meeting. The presence of a majority of the membership will constitute a quorum at any meeting.

Section 5.   At a meeting at which there is a quorum present, a simple majority affirmative vote of the directors present is required to pass a motion before the board.

Section 6.   Proxy voting _____ (will/will not) _____ be permitted.

Section 7.   Robert's Rules of Order will be the authority for all questions of procedure at any meetings of the corporation.

ARTICLE VI. OFFICERS

Section 1.   The officers of this corporation will be a president, vice-president, secretary, treasurer, and such other officers with duties as the board prescribes.

Section 2.   The officers of the corporation will be elected annually by the members of the board of directors at its annual meeting. Each officer will serve _____-year terms.

Section 3.   Any officer may be removed with or without cause by the board of directors by a vote of a majority of all of the board members. The matter of removal may be acted upon at any meeting of the board, provided that notice of intention to consider said removal has been given to each board member and to the officer affected at least _____ days previously.

Section 4.   A vacancy in any office may be filled by a majority vote of the board of directors for the unexpired portion of the term.

Section 5.   The *president* will be the chief executive officer of the corporation. It will be the duty of the president to preside at all meetings of the board of directors and to have general supervision of the affairs of the corporation. He or she will execute on behalf of the corporation all contracts, deeds, conveyances, and other instruments in writing that may be required or authorized by the board of directors for the proper and necessary transaction of the business of the corporation.

Section 6.   It will be the duty of the *vice-president* to act in the absence or disability of the president and to perform such other duties as may be assigned to him or her by the president or the board. In the absence of the president, the execution by the vice-president on behalf of the corporation of any instrument will have the same force and effect as if it were executed on behalf of the corporation by the president.

Section 7: The *secretary* will be responsible for keeping the corporate records. He or she will give or cause to be given all notices of meetings of the board of directors and all other notices required by law or by these bylaws. The secretary will be the custodian of all books, correspondence, and papers relating to the business of the corporation, except those of the treasurer. The secretary will present at each annual meeting of the board of directors a full report of the transactions and affairs of the corporation for the preceding year and will also prepare and present to the board of directors such other reports as it may desire and request at such time or times as it may designate. The board of directors at its discretion may elect an assistant secretary, *not necessarily a member of the board of directors*, who will perform the duties and assume the responsibilities of the secretary as above set forth under the general direction of the secretary or the president.

Section 8. The *treasurer* will have general charge of the finances of the corporation. When necessary and proper, he or she will endorse on behalf of the corporation all checks, drafts, notes, and other obligations and evidences of the payment of money to the corporation or coming into his or her possession; and he or she will deposit the same, together with all other funds of the corporation coming into his or her possession, in such bank or banks as may be selected by the board of directors. He or she will keep full and accurate account of all receipts and disbursements of the corporation in books belonging to the corporation, which will be open at all times to the inspection of the board of directors. He or she will present to the board of directors at its annual meeting his or her report as treasurer of the corporation and will from time to time make such other reports to the board of directors as it may require.

Section 9. Any officer of the corporation, in addition to the powers conferred upon him or her by these bylaws, will have such additional powers and perform such additional duties as may be prescribed from time to time by said board.

ARTICLE VII. COMMITTEES

Section 1. The board of directors may designate one or more ad hoc committees, each of which will consist of at least one committee chair and two or more committee members. Committee members may be members of the board of directors, members of the corporation, or other interested individuals. The chair of the committee will be appointed by the president of the organization, who will act with the board's approval. After consultation with the committee chair, the president will appoint committee members. The studies, findings, and recommendations of all committees will be reported to the board of directors for consideration and action, except as otherwise ordered by the board of directors. Committees may adopt such rules for the conduct of business as are appropriate and as are not inconsistent with these bylaws, the articles of incorporation, or state law.

Section 2. The board of directors will have the following standing committees.

Executive Committee: This committee will be chaired by the president of the corporation and will consist of all other officers of the corporation and the chairs of all other committees. This committee will serve as the central planning group for the organization and as an advisory group to the executive director. It also will have full authority to act for the board in managing the affairs of the corporation during the intervals between meetings of the board.

Budget and Finance: This committee will be chaired by the treasurer and will consist of _____ to _____ members appointed by the president to _____-year terms. This committee will oversee and monitor the fiscal operations of the organization, develop an annual budget for recommendation by the board, and develop and assist in the implementation of a funding strategy for the corporation.

ARTICLE VIII. MISCELLANEOUS

Section 1.   The corporation will have the power to indemnify and hold harmless any director, officer, or employee from any suit, damage, claim, judgment, or liability arising out of, or asserted to arise out of, conduct of such person in his or her capacity as a director, officer, or employee (except in cases involving willful misconduct). The corporation will have the power to purchase or procure insurance for such purposes.

Section 2.   The board of directors may authorize any officer or officers, agent or agents of the corporation, in addition to the officers so authorized by these bylaws, to enter into any contract or execute and deliver any instrument in the name of, and on behalf of, the corporation. Such authority may be general or confined to specific instances.

Section 3.   All checks, drafts, and other orders for payment of funds will be signed by such officers or such other persons as the board of directors may from time to time designate. All documents will require two such signatures, at least one of which must be that of a member of the board of directors and the other may be of the executive director.

Section 4.   The corporation will keep correct and complete books and records of account and will also keep minutes of the proceedings of its members, board of directors, and committees having any of the authority of the board of directors; and it will keep at the registered or principal office a record giving the names and addresses of the members entitled to vote. All books and records of the corporation may be inspected by any member or his or her agent or attorney for any proper purpose at any reasonable time.

Section 5.   The fiscal year of the corporation will be _____ through _____.

ARTICLE IX. AMENDMENTS

The board of directors may amend these bylaws to include or omit any provision that it could lawfully include or omit at the time the amendment is made. Upon written notice of at least _____ days, any number of amendments or an entire revision of the bylaws may be submitted and voted upon at a single meeting of the board of directors and will be adopted at such meeting upon receiving a _____ vote of the members of the board of directors.

ARTICLE X. DISSOLUTION

Upon the dissolution of the corporation and after the payment or the provision for payment of all the liabilities of the corporation, the board of directors will dispose of all of the assets of the corporation exclusively for the purposes of the corporation or to organizations that are then qualified as tax-exempt organizations under section 501(c)(3) of the Internal Revenue code. Any assets not so disposed of will be disposed of by a court of jurisdiction in the county in which the principal office of the corporation is located.

Legal Aspects:
Cutting the Red Tape

There are a variety of legal requirements that apply to nonprofit organizations. Such legal concerns include incorporation, tax exemption, bylaws, and other licensing and reporting requirements. Some of these concerns are governed by federal law, others by state law. Most of these procedures are fairly simple, once you understand them. Although it is possible to "go it on your own," it can be helpful, time saving, and reassuring to have the assistance of an attorney. There are attorneys who specialize in this area of law. Since attorneys' fees can be formidable, check to see whether you can get donated or inexpensive legal services through a legal assistance program or through contacts made by a board member.

INCORPORATION

It is not necessary for an organization to incorporate in order to function on a nonprofit basis. However, incorporation is highly advisable since incorporation as a nonprofit is the general rule for social service agencies and most arts and community interest groups and many people do not understand and will not deal with unincorporated organizations. The other major advantages of incorporating include limited liability of members, ongoing "corporate" existence, and facilitation of tax exemption.

What Does Incorporation Mean?

A *corporation* is a legal entity with rights, privileges, and liabilities separate from those of the individuals who compose its membership. A corporation can act, and the corporation—and not those who form it, invest money in it, or serve as its members—bears the responsibility for, and enjoys the benefits of, the actions it takes.

The corporation is the principal form of organization used for doing business in the United States. Even though a large number of businesses are sole proprietorships or partnerships, those doing the greatest volume of business and owning the most capital are organized in the corporate form. Incorporation is also a major form of organization for nonbusiness groups formed for artistic, educational, social, or charitable purposes. These groups are not formed to produce profits, but to provide a service to the community. Incorporated nonprofit organizations, therefore, do not have stockholders as do business corporations but, instead, have members who perform the stockholders' functions or a board of directors that performs both the stockholders' and the directors' functions.

Corporations are generally formed under the provisions of state law. Generally, there are separate statutes that govern incorporation procedures and requirements for nonprofit groups, including philanthropic, religious, social service, welfare, educational, patriotic, cultural, artistic, and public interest organizations. Formation of a corporation under such statutes creates a new entity with the following special characteristics and powers.

1. **Limited Liability**: The most important advantage of incorporation is the limited liability of its members. In other words, the individuals who control the corporation are not responsible, except in unusual situations, for the legal and financial obligations of the organization. Corporations can incur debts as a result of purchases, salary expenses, building mortgages, and service contracts. They can have legal obligations resulting from contracts. These debts and obligations are in the name of the corporation rather than in the names of the individuals who are its members. This reduces the risk to individuals involved in group ventures.

   There can be exceptions to the rule of limited liability in cases in which the courts believe that the members or the directors have not tried in good faith to conduct the business of the corporation in a responsible manner. In order to ensure their limited liability, members and directors should (1) make it clear when they are conducting the agency's business that they are doing so on behalf of the corporation, (2) make sure that the agency's funds are kept separate from the funds of individuals, (3) hold regular meetings to review and conduct corporate business, and (4) make an effort to secure sufficient funds for the corporation.

2. **Continuity**: A corporation will continue to exist "perpetually" until legal dissolution unless it is chartered for only a specified, limited period of time. Its legal existence is not dependent on the continued participation of individual members or directors.

3. **Uniform Set of Rules**: Because the operation of corporations is governed by a uniform, though flexible, set of rules under state law, those involved in corporations and those who deal with them know how they should operate and what should be expected of them. For example, it is relatively easy to prove that the officers of a corporation are, in fact, authorized to enter into a contract on behalf of the corporation. It would be much more difficult to prove that individuals acting on behalf of an unincorporated organization are authorized to enter into a contract for the organization. As a consequence, most businesses, fundors, and banks prefer to deal only with incorporated nonprofit organizations.

4. **Tax Exemption**: An important reason for incorporation is that it facilitates getting tax-exempt status under federal and state income tax laws. A copy of the articles of incorporation must be filed with a request for federal tax exemption.

How Does an Organization Incorporate?

A nonprofit organization becomes a corporation by (1) selecting a name for the organization that is not being used by any other incorporated group in the state, (2) drafting the legal incorporation document, or articles of incorporation, and filing it with the state, and (3) holding the first official meeting of the board to adopt bylaws and elect officers. Legal assistance in filing for incorporation is advisable but not necessary. In many cases, an attorney may simply review the articles of incorporation after the organizers complete the form.

Check your state's law on the minimum number of persons needed to act as incorporators. In Minnesota, for instance, at least three of legal age (eighteen or older) may form a corporation. In choosing a name for your corporation, check with the secretary of state's office to make sure that the same or a similar name is not being used by another group within the state.

The secretary of state also can supply a form for the articles of incorporation. This form can be used as is, or it can be used as a guide to formulating your own articles of incorporation (for instance, in a case in which more space is needed than is provided on the form).

The information required for the articles of incorporation generally includes the following items.

1. The name of the corporation.
2. The purpose of the corporation.
3. A statement that the corporation does not afford "pecuniary gain," or profit, to its members.
4. The period of duration of corporate existence, which may be perpetual.
5. The location, by city or community, of its registered office.
6. The name and address of each incorporator.
7. The number of directors constituting the first board of directors, the name and address of each director, and the tenure in office of the first directors.
8. The extent of personal liability, if any, of members for corporate obligations and the methods of enforcement and collection (there will be none, except in unusual circumstances).
9. Whether the corporation has capital stock (most nonprofit corporations do not have capital stock).
10. Provisions for the distribution of corporate assets and for dissolution.
11. Whether or not there will be a membership separate from the board of directors. A statement that membership is the board of directors is advantageous for nonmembership organizations. Without such a statement, it could be assumed that the corporation has a separate membership that elects the board of directors.

When they are complete, the articles of incorporation are submitted to the office of the secretary of state. A certificate of incorporation will be issued by the secretary of state; at that time, the corporation legally begins its existence. The articles will be filed with the secretary of state and the county registrar of deeds, and the certificate of incorporation will be sent to the organization within a couple of weeks.

After the organization's incorporation, the first meeting of the directors should be held. During the first meeting, the initial bylaws are adopted, the officers are elected, and any other business is conducted. This meeting is mandatory. State law requires that nonprofit corporations have bylaws and conduct themselves in a certain manner and within certain structural limitations (such as having a board of directors, officers, periodic meetings, financial records and minutes, et cetera). For membership organizations, the law sets out various requirements that are assumed unless stated otherwise in the bylaws. If the organization desires a relatively small, closed base, the "board equals members" concept should be considered. Should community involvement be desired at some later time, the bylaws could be revised to provide for an advisory board or another such body.

In Minnesota, incorporation falls under the provisions of the Nonprofit Corporation Act, chapter 317 of the Minnesota statutes. The articles of incorporation form for nonprofit organizations is available from the office of the secretary of state.

TAX EXEMPTION

In addition to forming a nonprofit corporation, you must also be designated as tax-exempt in order to be "fundable." Your tax-exempt status frees your fundors from paying taxes on the money they donate to your organization. And, of course, your nonprofit organization will not be taxed on its income. Once the corporation has been formed, it can apply for tax-exempt status from both federal and state governments.

Federal Tax Exemption

Tax exemption is granted by the Internal Revenue Service (IRS) to nonprofit corporations performing charitable, educational, scientific, religious, or cultural activities under section 501(c)(3) of the Internal Revenue code of 1954, as amended.

Some types of nonprofit organizations, those making a major effort to influence legislation, may be classified under section 501(c)(4) rather than under 501(c)(3). Contributions to 501(c)(4) tax-exempt organizations may not be claimed as charitable contributions on the income tax returns of the donors. However, 501(c)(3) organizations may also engage in lobbying, or attempting to influence legislation, to a limited degree. As a rule of thumb, 501(c)(3) organizations may spend up to 20 percent of their annual expenditures on lobbying; however, it is suggested that you seek legal advice regarding your organization's particular situation.

Applications for tax-exempt status should be made within fifteen months from the end of the month in which the organization was created, or incorporated; otherwise, the organization may be liable for taxes on income during the period prior to notification by the Internal Revenue Service of tax-exempt status. You should contact your local Internal Revenue Service office and ask for form 1023 (the application for applying for 501(c)(3) tax-exempt status) and the Internal Revenue Service publication 557 (the detailed instructions for determining your eligibility).

In addition to filing form 1023 for tax-exempt status, every exempt organization is required to have an employer identification number, whether or not it has any employees. An employer identification number is the official identification code for an organization (similar to a social security number for an individual) that is used by the Internal Revenue Service for tax-related purposes. To ensure the quickest validation for tax-exempt status from the Internal Revenue Service, you should file for the employer idenitification number with form SS-4 simultaneously with form 1023. Both forms can be obtained from a local Internal Revenue Service office.

You can file the application yourself, but it is generally better to have the assistance of an attorney. Copies of your articles of incorporation and your bylaws should be included with the application. The Internal Revenue Service responds to the application with a letter that states that the organization is tax-exempt and cites the exact code under which it is classified. It can take up to three months for the Internal Revenue Service to respond to your application, but it usually takes only a few weeks. A copy of this letter should accompany most of your organization's major fund-raising proposals.

Within five and one-half months after the end of each fiscal year, tax-exempt 501(c)(3) organizations must file form 990, the return of organizations exempt from income tax, with the Internal Revenue Service. This form requires an accounting of all income, expenses, assets, and liabilities of the organization.

State Tax Exemption

After receiving federal tax-exempt status, nonprofit corporations should apply for exemption from state income taxes. The procedure for filing for state income tax exemption is routine since the state usually follows the ruling of the Internal Revenue Service. State tax exemption is granted by state departments of revenue.

To apply for state tax exemption for your organization in Minnesota, you should request form 120-A from the Department of Revenue. Along with the completed 120-A form, send copies of your organization's letter of determination for federal tax-exempt status and of your bylaws to the Minnesota Department of Revenue. It should take only a week or two to receive notice of state tax-exempt status.

Once your organization has received tax-exempt status from the Minnesota Department of Revenue, contact with that office continues annually. Organizations filing income tax form 990 with the Internal Revenue Service should also file annually a copy of their 990 with the Minnesota Department of Revenue. Again, this procedure is only routine and is just another one of those compliance rulings an incorporated organization must follow according to the law.

The procedures for obtaining tax exemptions in other states are similar. Contact your state department of revenue for application forms and further information.

State Sales Tax Exemption

In most states, sales tax is levied on luxury items sold to the general public (in retail sales). However, most nonprofit corporations are exempt from paying taxes on any goods.

In order for a nonprofit corporation to purchase goods without paying the sales tax, the purchasers must provide the seller with a tax-exemption number. This number, known as a certificate of exempt status, can be applied for from the state department of revenue. (To apply for sales tax-exempt status in Minnesota, file form ST-16 with the Minnesota Department of Revenue.) Once your organization has received its sales tax-exempt number, it is your responsibility to present the number at the time of purchase to enjoy the privilege of sales tax exemption. To receive tax-exemption forms, instructions, and general information, contact the nearest office of your state department of revenue.

Utilities Tax Exemption

Organizations that qualify for federal and state tax exemption do not have to pay taxes on telephone or other utility bills. Contact your telephone company representative for more information and to inform them of your exemption. If you pay your own gas and electricity bills, these companies should be informed of the tax exemption for your organization, also.

Social Security Exemption

The Federal Insurance Contribution Act (FICA) was set up to assist workers during retirement through social security benefits. Each employee and employer is expected to contribute money to the fund in order to pay benefits for presently retired workers. The contribution rate of 6.13 percent of the first $25,900 of an employee's salary is contributed by both the employee and the employer for a total rate of 12.26 percent of an individual's salary. This contribution rate will increase in the near future. Ask a local Social Security Administration office for the current rates.

Contributing to Federal Insurance Contribution Act, which is more commonly known as social security, is optional for nonprofit organizations. In fact, 501(c)(3) organizations are automatically exempt from contributing. The decision about whether or not to contribute to social security is made by the employing unit as a whole rather than by the individual employees. Thus, contributing to the fund is on an either/or basis for the nonprofit organization; either everyone contributes to the fund or no one does. New, small nonprofits usually choose not to participate in the Federal Insurance Contribution Act. Low salaries and a tight budget are two reasons organizations elect to take advantage of the exemption. However, it is important to remember that the decision not to contribute to social security is not final. At any time the employees, the executive director, and the board of directors feel financially comfortable with contributing to the fund, they can do so.

If your organization chooses to contribute to social security, simply request form SS-15A from your local Internal Revenue Service or Social Security Administration office and complete the form, providing the names, social security numbers, and signatures of the organization's employees.

State Unemployment Insurance

Most states have an unemployment insurance program designed to aid those who are temporarily unemployed. These programs are generally supported through an employer tax on all groups and businesses, including nonprofit corporations, who employ residents within the state. Check with your state department of employment services to find out whether there is such a tax, whether it applies to your organization, and what procedures should be followed if there is such a tax.

The Minnesota Unemployment Insurance program, for example, is set up to benefit unemployed workers by having the state pay an unemployed person, depending upon the worker's number of dependents and past work experience, a certain percentage of his or her most recent salary. If an unemployed worker is eligible, he or she will receive compensation from a fund that is contributed to by each employer. Employees do not contribute to the fund. Employers contribute to the Minnesota Unemployment Compensation Fund according to rates determined by the amount of claims unemployed workers have filed against an employer. The fewer workers filing for unemployment benefits against an individual employing unit, the less the rate charged by the Department of Employment Services.

The rates charged in Minnesota vary from 2.5 percent to 7.5 percent on the first $7,000 of an employee's salary. All employees, including temporary and part-time workers, are equally considered by the Department of Employment Services when the tax is levied. In order for the state to determine your experience rating for a year, form MES-13, the report to determine liability, must be filed before your corporate operations start with the Department of Employment Services. The department will automatically assign you a rating each year, depending on the past year's record of claims.

The employing unit must file quarterly contribution reports (MES-1) and pay taxes on the wages reported. The quarterly contribution report and taxes are due within one month after the end of a calendar quarter, in other words, on April 30, July 31, October 31, and January 31. A new employer is expected to notify the State Department of Employment Services within thirty days following the beginning of operations. The employer is required to maintain complete records on each employee, which show the amount worked, the wages paid, and the service performed.

Contact your state department of economic security for more specific information regarding unemployment compensation.

All nonprofit, tax-exempt organizations described in section 501(c)(3) of the Federal Internal Revenue code are exempt from contributions to the federal government's Unemployment Insurance Contribution Fund.

STATE AND LOCAL REGISTRATION REQUIREMENTS

State and local laws may also require other types of registration for nonprofit organizations. A state department of commerce may regulate their activities. Cities may require permits for groups raising funds within their boundaries. Groups organizing as nonprofit corporations should check with the secretary of state, department of commerce, and department of revenue in their state to determine which regulations apply to them. Although the following information applies to organizations within the state of Minnesota nonprofits in other states should check for similar state and local requirements.

Registration with Minnesota Department of Commerce

Minnesota law requires registration and reports from the following nonprofit organizations: (1) those soliciting $10,000 or more per year from "public" sources, including foundations and individuals other than members; (2) those paying a professional fund raiser; or (3) those soliciting under $10,000 per year but employing a paid staff or other workers. These organizations must file a registration statement and a financial report with the charities section of the Department of Commerce within thirty days after the date on which their publicly solicited contributions reach $10,000. Those paying a staff or a fund raiser should register when they hire their personnel.

Each year, registered organizations must file a two-page annual report form and a financial statement within six months after the close of an organization's annual accounting period. If the organization fails to file an annual report and a financial statement on time, the registration statement will no longer be effective. Therefore, if problems arise that will delay the filing of an annual report or financial statement, the organization should notify the Department of Commerce and request an extension. Forms for the registration statement, the annual report, and the financial statement are available from the charities section of the Minnesota Department of Commerce. This unit also licenses all professional fund raisers who are hired on a consulting basis by nonprofit organizations.

In addition to the filing requirements outlined above, there are two other rules regulating nonprofit charitable organizations in Minnesota: (1) organizations raising more than $25,000 in a year must submit an audit statement signed by a certified public accountant with their annual reports, and (2) in order to maintain its tax-exempt status under Minnesota law, an organization is not to spend more than 30 percent of its total annual revenue for management and fund-raising costs.

Minnesota Charities Review Council

The Minnesota Charities Review Council is a private nonprofit corporation that serves as a kind of "better business bureau" for nonprofit charitable organizations. Its purpose is to investigate agencies that have been questioned by Minnesota citizens. It does not review every nonprofit organization in the state, only those about which it receives complaints or questions.

In such cases, the council requests information, primarily financial, from the organization, the state, and the city (if registration is required by the municipality), and then it makes this information available to the public. The Charities Review Council has no formal authority, but its close working relationship with the charities section of the Department of Commerce indirectly gives the council's reports considerable weight.

Public Solicitation Licenses

A few municipalities in Minnesota require nonprofit organizations that intend to solicit funds within their limits to file for a permit, or solicitation license. (Ordinances of this type do not apply to those organizations soliciting from their own members only.) Solicitation licenses generally must be acquired each year and require annual reports of income, expenses related to solicitations, and expenditures of the organization.

Nonprofit organizations soliciting ten or more sources in Minneapolis within a year (including corporations, foundations, or individuals) are required by the city to file for a solicitation license, with an annual fee of forty-nine dollars. In St. Paul, only those organizations that seek donations from individuals on the street are required to obtain a permit.

If you plan a large funding campaign aimed toward several sources within one municipality, you probably should check with the city clerk to see whether a solicitation license is required.

Bibliography

Nonprofit Corporations, Organizations, and Associations. By Howard Oleck. Englewood Cliffs, N.J.: Prentice-Hall, 1974. An in-depth "encyclopedia" of nonprofit corporation law, a useful reference for attorneys who work with nonprofit agencies. Covers incorporation, procedures for organization and management, guidelines for board proceedings, tax considerations, and rules and regulations pertaining to philanthropy. (1,000 pages)

Minnesota Nonprofit Corporations: A Corporate and Tax Guide. By John Hibbs. St. Paul: Minnesota Continuing Legal Education, 1979. A compilation of the principal corporate, tax, and other rules that apply in organizing, obtaining tax exemption for, operating, and dissolving most types of nonprofit corporations in Minnesota. (225 pages)

Program Planning:
Creating the Formula

"Cheshire-Puss," she began, "would you tell me, please, which way I ought to go from here?"

"That depends a good deal on where you want to get to," said the Cat.

"I don't care much where—" said Alice.

"Then it doesn't matter which way you go," said the Cat.

Without a well-thought-out plan, including clearly defined goals and objectives, there is no real basis for designing your program's content and selecting your methods. Neither is there a basis for judging whether your program has achieved what it was designed to do. "In other words," according to Robert Mager (*Goal Analysis*), "first decide where you want to go, then you create and administer the means of getting there, and then you arrange to find out whether you arrived. . . . In short, if you know where you are going, you have a better chance of getting there."

The program plan provides the basis for determining what resources are needed, for writing proposals, and for reviewing the actual performance of the program after it has been implemented. Most important, the plan directs the program as it progresses.

The program-planning process should be undertaken by an organization at various stages of its development: during the early stages of initial program development, when old services are being modified or new ones added, and at regular intervals (one- to three-year periods), when current plans are reviewed and directions for the upcoming period are decided upon.

Although there are several models of planning processes, most include the elements of the outline presented in the following pages. Program planning should include most, if not all, of these steps. Review this outline and develop a planning process that best suits the needs of your organization.

STEP 1: DETERMINE THE PROJECT IDEA

Generally, the overall purpose and design of a program has been decided before the program is actually planned. For instance, a community group may know that they want to deal with the "problem" of preventing delinquent behavior in elementary school children. Another may have organized to bring arts to their rural community. Although such groups have a vaguely defined purpose, or mission, they do not have a program. However, they have taken the first step.

At this stage, it is not necessary for the project idea to be clearly defined. In fact, its lack of definition can be an advantage in that it allows the planning group the freedom to examine a variety of approaches to, and perspectives on, the problem. The end point of the first planning step should be the development of a "mission statement." The *purpose*, or *mission, statement* describes the organization at its best; it puts forth the organization's highest aspirations. It is a broadly defined description of the purpose of the organization and the organization's activities. The mission may describe a state that may be impossible to achieve completely but one that encompasses the direction or thrust of the program. It generally speaks to a target population and a target need and may also speak to the program's service categories.

Examples

1. *To improve family relationships by increasing the parenting skills of parents and families in Cedarville.*
2. *To increase the skills of unemployed and underemployed women in Hennepin county in the areas of skill assessment, job application, and career development in order to improve their employment opportunities.*
3. *To promote natural resources and wilderness conservation throughout the state of Wisconsin.*

STEP 2: ASSESS THE NEED FOR THE PROJECT AND DEFINE THE PROBLEM

The next step in the planning process is to study the present conditions related to the problem and to identify the needs the program will address.

List and examine the problems related to your general purpose and their causes. Brainstorm as a group to determine as many related problem areas as possible. Be sure to identify the core problems as well as the more easily defined peripheral problems. Identify the needs the organization should consider addressing. Consider inviting members of the potential client group and others from related services to attend the problem-identification sessions.

Gather data to substantiate perceived problems. Often, the initial list of problems and needs is based on the subjective assessments and personal experiences of the planners. Objective data is necessary to confirm these assessments in order to ensure that your program addresses actual needs and to build a case in your program proposal for potential fundors. Such data are available from several sources. Use several of the following methods to assess the needs for your proposed program.

1. Collect pertinent census and other statistical data regarding population, age group distribution, income, ethnic distribution of population, educational levels, crime incidence, health information, and housing information. Such information is available from local and state law-enforcement agencies, health departments, and planning units.

2. Survey the personnel of existing programs working in the same problem areas to determine whether they believe that the proposed program is needed.

3. Survey a randomly selected number of citizens in the community or of potential clients to determine whether they perceive the need for such a service.

4. Contact community groups and community leaders to determine their impressions of the need for your program. Depending on your program and community, such leaders may include business people, politicians, members of the clergy, fundors, representatives of government or private agencies, and members and leaders of relevant community groups.

5. Survey the related literature in professional and general-interest journals and any local reports or studies on the topic. Use the information and recommendations generated by studies.

6. Contact the constituencies of existing programs to determine whether they see a need for other services.

The results of this needs assessment may not totally support your original perception of the problem. You may need to redefine the problem as a result of this data-gathering process.

Identify the specific concerns and define the target audience on which the organization will focus. From the initial list of problems, select those that your program realistically *can* work on, given practical limitations. What situations can you have an impact on? Decide which of these your program *will* address. (There will always be aspects of a problem over which you can have no control or influence.) In addition, select and define your target client population. For instance, a program should be designed not for "youths" but for a specific group of youth, such as youths aged twelve to eighteen in a specific neighborhood who are identified as using drugs extensively or inappropriately. The better you are able to define the target audience, the more likely that the program will be effective in meeting the needs of its clients. As a result of this process, you should develop a problem statement and a defined client population. Although these terms are most used in social services, other types of organizations—arts, advocacy, religious, educational, et cetera—can develop similar statements regarding needs and constituencies addressed.

Examples

1.   Problem Statement: *Many elderly citizens in the community are forced to give up living independently because they lack transportation, are unable to perform heavy housekeeping and maintenance tasks, and no longer have regular personal or family contacts.*
2.   Client Population: *Residents in the downtown neighborhood over age sixty-five who live independently but who need assistance to continue living in their own homes or apartments.*

STEP 3: DETERMINE THE CAPACITY FOR IMPACT ON THE PROBLEM AND IDENTIFY THE FACTORS THAT LIMIT THE CAPACITY

How reasonable is it to expect that you can bring about a favorable change in the problem you have defined? What are the factors in your favor? What are the forces working for the continuation of the defined problem? The planning process must include a realistic assessment of the extent to which your program can have an impact on the problem.

Identify the factors that could help you to address the problem. These could include available financial and manpower resources, community support, legislative concerns, support of key people, existing programs related to problem, and favorable attitudes among your constituency.

Identify the factors external to your program that could limit your impact on the problem. These could include lack of financial and community support, negative factors in the community or population that are difficult or impossible to control, and lack of support of key people. Some factors can be addressed by your program. Are there facilitating factors that could be implemented to counteract these? After you have considered these variables, determine which strategies could (1) eliminate or weaken those factors that limit your efforts, (2) strengthen the facilitating factors, or (3) do a combination of 1 and 2.

STEP 4: IDENTIFY THE UNDERLYING ASSUMPTIONS AND VALUES OF THE PLANNING GROUP

What are the premises about human behavior, the attitudes and the principles that will form the basis of the program? Although in many groups and programs these assumptions are unspoken, they are always present, directly influencing program format and outcome. Just as the problem-related data provides the *objective* answer to the question "why this program?" these assumptions and value statements are your *subjective* response to the question. If you are conscious of these assumptions, you can use them positively to develop your program and you can eliminate assumptions that may not be valid or those upon which the planning group does not agree. Discuss and identify your assumptions and values as a group. Although there may not be total agreement, the planning group should be able to reach a consensus about the underlying assumptions of the program you propose.

Examples

1. *Education about nutrition will improve eating habits.*
2. *Alcoholism is a disease that patients can control.*
3. *Children benefit educationally and emotionally from contact with the arts.*

STEP 5: DEVELOP THE GOALS AND OBJECTIVES FOR THE PROGRAM

Goals and objectives define the intended outcomes of the project. They are concise statements of what the program is designed to accomplish. Goals describe longer term, broader final results, whereas objectives describe shorter term results necessary for the completion of a goal.

A *goal* is a description of a new condition that the program will achieve through the services provided. A program generally has only a few goals, which specify each of the intended results. Goals must be realistic and achievable. They should be within the control of those responsible for accomplishing them. They should be consistent with the statement of the organization's purpose.

Goals are generally broad in scope, based on long-term aims, and stated in terms of measurable criteria. The results, and not the process, of the program are the focus of the goals. In other words, goals should describe, not your programs, but the changes that will result from these programs.

Examples

1. *To provide parenting education to pregnant teens.* (Poor)
   To increase the parenting skills of each client who completes the program. (Better)
2. *To bring cultural activities to our community.* (Poor)
   To increase the accessibility of our community to theater, art, film, and music. (Better)

Objectives are the measurable accomplishments or changes required to create the new conditions specified in each of the goals. Each objective makes a partial contribution to the realization of a goal. There may be several objectives per goal. When all of the objectives have been accomplished, the goal has been met.

Objectives should be specific as to outcome, degree of change, population, and deadline. For each objective, or projected outcome, ask yourself the following questions.

1. *Who* will be affected?
2. *What* is going to change (attitudes, knowledge, behavior)?
3. *When* will the change occur?
4. *How much* change, in *how many* people, does the program plan to produce?
5. *What* will be the *indicator* of such change (observable behavior, test results, et cetera)?

Objectives are more specific than goals and break down broad goals into smaller components that describe more narrowly defined achievements. They contain more exact measurement references related to anticipated achievement levels. Often, precise estimates regarding performance will be projected. It is important that these projected "success" rates are realistic and, if possible, that they are based on the experience of similar programs.

Like goals, objectives focus on results rather than methods. For instance, they describe what changes will occur in client behavior rather than the services provided to clients. Like goals, objectives should be feasible, measurable, and clearly understandable by anyone.

The following are examples of objectives that relate to the sample goal of the program for pregnant teens.

Examples

1. *Each client will demonstrate appropriate infant care techniques as listed in the "Infant Care Checklist" during daily sessions at the nursery.*
2. *After four months in the program, at least 80 percent of the clients will achieve a minimum score of seventy on an oral or written test designed to measure knowledge of infant development.*
3. *By the time the program has been completed, each participant will be able to identify five to eight community resources or agencies available to help young mothers in areas such as child care, health, family planning, income maintenance, vocational training, and counseling.*

It is important that goals and objectives be *measurable*. If you cannot measure how well you have achieved your goals and objectives, you may not be sure you have accomplished anything or produced any of the results you intended. The measurement included in objectives may be results on pretests and posttests or questionnaires, observable behavior (pregnancy, court adjudication, legislation passed), or simply the number of people participating in a program.

Whenever the performance stated in an objective is abstract or covert (internal, mental), add an overt behavior to the objective that is measurable or observable that might indicate whether the covert performance has been achieved.

Although goals and objectives can form a sturdy framework for program planners, many planners choose not to differentiate between the two. Instead, they describe their program plan in a series of goal/objective statements that may be either short- or long-term. You must decide which format works best for you.

If you choose to use goal/objective statements rather than to separate your broader long-term and more specific short-term aims, be sure that these statements describe measurable outcomes. These outcome statements refer specifically to who will be affected; describe what these people are expected to do, under what conditions, and how well or to what extent; and include a time factor.

Goals and objectives need to be written clearly and simply, in terms free of jargon and ambiguity that can be easily understood by anyone, within or outside the organization.

STEP 6: CHOOSE METHODS AND OUTLINE THE WORK PLAN

You have finally reached the stage at which you are ready to plan the services your program will offer. How will you accomplish your objectives? What methods, activities, or treatment plan will result in the outcomes you have planned?

Determine the overall program approach. A helpful first step is brainstorming about all of the possible strategies that relate to your goals and objectives. What approaches to this problem have been tried in the past? With what results? Are any particular strategies suggested by pertinent research or literature? Are there any similar programs in your own community or in other areas on which you want to model your program? If other projects addressing this problem have not been successful, how will your program be different? What approach is most feasible, in terms of your resources, values, and goals? Which strategies will overcome the limiting factors and strengthen the facilitating factors you have identified previously? Which methods are most likely to be supported by funding sources? Which would be most acceptable to your target population or constituency? From these possibilities, your planning group must select an approach to the problem that is feasible, consistent with your values and beliefs, appropriate for your "audience," and likely to achieve the desired outcome.

Decide which activities you will undertake in your approach in order to address each of the program's goals and objectives. What services will you offer to achieve the desired outcomes? Activities should be stated in terms of specific actions to be taken: provide counseling, deliver meals to the homebound, teach parenting skills, sponsor cultural events, lobby for environmental causes. Describe these activities as specifically as possible. Each activity should be matched to the objective that it supports. (An activity can relate to more than one objective.)

Each activity should be put into a time frame. When will it start? How long will it take? How often will it be done? When will it be completed? An activity calendar can then be formulated that will serve as the work plan for the organization.

be assigned to staff members or others. vity? Who else will contribute to it? This he job descriptions for each of the staff ess, you should have developed a written ving items.

s to be conducted.
2. A description of the treatment methods to be used (if applicable).
3. A calendar of the tasks required to achieve the objectives.
4. A list of task assignments.
5. Preliminary outlines of job descriptions.

STEP 7: IDENTIFY THE RESOURCES NECESSARY TO PERFORM THE ACTIVITIES

Examine the work plan and determine what resources the organization must have to carry it out. (This task will be much easier when you have kept monetary limitations in mind when designing your goals, objectives, and work plan!)

Determine the size and skills of the staff needed to provide these services.

Determine what size and structure is necessary for office and program space as well as what furnishings and equipment are required.

Determine what other resources will be necessary to support the program (office supplies, printing facilities, postage, et cetera) and the staff (conferences, publications, et cetera).

This list will form the basis for developing the program budget. (See the chapter on budgets for more extensive information on determining the monetary values of resources needed.)

STEP 8: DESIGN AN EVALUATION SYSTEM TO MONITOR THE PROGRAM'S EFFECTIVENESS

An evaluation system is the means by which an organization determines the impact of its program on the problem areas on which it focuses. It is important for evaluation purposes that goals and objectives are measurable. If your program is doing things that cannot be evaluated or measured, you may be unable to demonstrate that you are achieving anything.

Choose the criteria by which you will judge whether your goals and objectives have been achieved. How will you differentiate those clients who have achieved the goal from those who have not? How will you know whether your activities achieved their purpose? There are several common ways to measure outcomes, including the following.

1. Counting the number of people served.
2. Using appropriate tests or questionnaires at intake and program completion to measure changes in attitudes and/or knowledge.
3. Comparing reported behavior before and after program involvement (through health records, court records, self-reporting, reporting by professionals or other family members.)
4. Surveying participants (and their families and/or concerned professionals—teachers, counselors, et cetera) to determine satisfaction with program.
5. Comparing those served with others from the target population who did not receive your services (interesting to do but usually very difficult).

Choose methods appropriate for each objective. Use more than one means of measurement when possible.

Develop means of recording observable changes. This relates directly to the measurement methods chosen and can include designing forms, developing surveys and questionnaires, choosing appropriate tests, et cetera. These can be developed by the staff alone or with the aid of an outside consultant.

Decide on a reporting system. The data gathered from the various records kept by the organization should form the basis of quarterly and annual reports. The reports should relate directly to the goals and objectives in your program plan, and they should provide a means for comparing achievements to planned performance. Decide who will be responsible for designing forms, maintaining records, and reporting. You may wish to consider getting the assistance of an outside consultant during any or all of these stages. Remember to include any proposed consultant fees in the program budget. The program plan, then, also serves as an evaluation tool. It tells you where you are going, how you will get there, and how you will know when you have arrived.

STEP 9: IMPLEMENT THE WORK PLAN AND MONITOR THE PROGRAM'S IMPACT

After the program plan has been completed, recheck the plan. Is it complete? Is it consistent? Is it what you want to do? Is it possible for you to do? Make any changes necessary to ensure that it is. The plan is not worth your time and effort if it is not something you are going to use.

Two common and critical mistakes are often made by program planners and staff after developing written goals and objectives and a work plan: (1) they file them in the back of a dusty, unused drawer and ignore them, or (2) they follow them slavishly, ignoring indications of the need to change the plans.

The program plan should be used as a guide during the implementation of your program. Monitor your program's progress through the collection of evaluative data and by the periodic review of "where you're at" in terms of your original plan.

At these periodic review points (perhaps quarterly), determine whether any changes are called for in goals, objectives, or methods. When the initial program period is over, you should be able to determine whether you have achieved your intended results. You should also be able to determine whether the initial program plan was a good one.

STEP 10: REVIEW THE PROGRAM PLAN AND REPEAT THE PLANNING PROCESS

At this point, the planning cycle begins again. After the first year of implementation, review your program plan. Was it realistic? Did you achieve what you wanted to? Why not? What changes should be made?

Every program should renew itself on a regular basis by redefining its program plan through steps 5–9 of the planning process. After longer periods of time, the program should be reexamined, beginning with steps 1–4.

USING THE PLANNING MODEL

This process, in practice, is not as rigid as it appears on paper. Planning groups should examine this model and consider how it can best be applied to their own organization. In some cases, it will be frustrating to try to quantify the objectives of your program. Some of your program's accomplishments cannot be counted, measured, and pinpointed. Nevertheless, it is important to try to measure, as specifically as possible, the outcomes of your program. A well-designed program plan gives an organization a clear destination and a way to tell whether it got there.

The blueprint for program planning that follows can be used for outlining core program plans during steps two, four, five and six.

A BLUEPRINT FOR PROGRAM PLANNING

PROBLEMS	GOALS	OBJECTIVES	METHODS
Problem statements briefly describe situations that are seen by program planners as having a negative impact on the community.	*Goals* are descriptions of new conditions that the program will bring about, related to the described problems. They describe long-term outcomes. Goals must be realistic (considering the current situation and resources of the agency), precise, and significantly challenging to the agency.	*Objectives* are the measurable accomplishments or changes required to create the new conditions specified in each of the goals. Each goal may have several related objectives. Objectives should specify what will change, among whom, when, and how much change will occur. Like goals, objectives focus on results rather than on methods.	*Methods* are the processes and activities that will be used to meet the objectives. These become the program and service description of your agency.
EXAMPLE: There is an increase in the number of teenage mothers choosing to keep their children. These mothers are generally unprepared for parenting.	EXAMPLE: To increase the parenting skills of pregnant teenage clients.	EXAMPLE: Each client will demonstrate appropriate infant care techniques as listed in the "Infant Care Checklist" during weekly session in the nursery.	EXAMPLE: Clients will participate in daily sessions with infants in the nursery and will receive instructions and education in infant care.

ASSUMPTIONS

Assumptions are the values, philosophies, and premises about human behavior that serve as a basis for program development.

EXAMPLE: With training and support, teens can be adequate parents.

A BLUEPRINT FOR PROGRAM PLANNING

PROBLEMS	GOALS	OBJECTIVES	METHODS

ASSUMPTIONS

Bibliography

Assessing Human Needs. League of California Cities, 702 Hilton Center, Los Angeles, Cal., 90017, 1975. Stresses the use of needs assessment in long-range planning, setting measurable objectives, targeting services to a specific population, and allocating staff and financial resources. Describes how to carry out a needs assessment. (167 pages)

Community Needs and Resources Assessment Guidebook. National Center for Voluntary Action, 1214 16th Street N.W., Washington, D.C. 20036, 1976. Outlines process for conducting needs assessments, based on developing an inventory of existing and needed programs. (32 pages)

Goal Analysis. By Robert Mager. San Francisco: Fearon Publications, 1972. Explains how to define fuzzy, broad goals in terms of performances that represent goal achievement. Teaches distinction between performances and abstractions. (136 pages)

How to Deal with Goals and Objectives. By L. L. Morris and C. T. Fitz-Gibbon. Beverly Hills, Cal.: Sage Publications, 1978. Covers developing goals, writing behavioral objectives, and assigning priorities to objectives. Aimed at educators, but useful for others developing goals and objectives. (78 pages)

Planning for a Change. By Duane Dale and Nancy Mitiguy. Citizen Involvement Training Project, University of Massachusetts, Amherst, Mass., 1978. Excellent guide for program planning. Topics include planning models, idea generation, force field analysis, brainstorming, assessment of optional program ideas, program implementation, and evaluation. Practical case studies and exercises are included. (88 pages)

Playing Their Game Our Way: Using the Political Process to Meet Community Needs. By Greg Speeter. Citizen Involvement Training Program, University of Massachusetts, Amherst, Mass., 1978. Geared toward groups advocating issues through lobbying and other political activities. Outlines planning strategy for such groups. Includes exercises and specific suggestions. Excellent resource for community groups who work in the political arena with the "big guys." (120 pages)

Preparing Instructional Objectives. By Robert Mager. San Francisco: Fearon Publications, 1962. One of the best books on how to write objectives. Although it is oriented toward education, it is just as applicable to the writing of program objectives. (60 pages)

Budget Development:
Adding Up the Bill

How much is it going to cost you to do what you want to do? How much income do you anticipate raising and from where? If you do your job well, the answers to these questions should be found in your budget.

The budget is the financial blueprint of your organization. It is an outline of the anticipated expenses and income of the organization during a specific period, usually a year. (The annual twelve-month period used for financial planning purposes is called a fiscal year. This need not correspond to the calendar year, January through December.) The budget is an educated guess about all of the money needed to run your programs and about where that money will come from. (The better educated the guess, the more useful the budget!) A budget is today's plan for the cost of operating tomorrow's program.

Expenditures listed in the budget generally include salaries, employee benefits, rent and utilities, equipment and supplies, and any other expected costs. Although many budgets include only expenditures, it is useful to include an outline of anticipated income—grants, contracts, contributions, fees, and donations of services and supplies—as well.

HOW IS A BUDGET USED?

The most immediate usefulness of the budget is in the area of fund raising. You need to know how much money you must raise in order to conduct your program for at least a one-year period before you can determine where this money will come from. A budget is essential to your funding proposal. The funds your program requires should be projected clearly on paper so that the organization's needs can be understood by potential fundors. The budget is also an indication to fundors of your planning and management skills.

However, don't make the mistake of hanging your budget at the end of your proposal and forgetting it! It was not developed only for the files of your fundors. Your budget should be used as an ongoing management tool by the program director, staff, and board of directors. If you shelve it until the end of your fiscal year, you may find that you are having difficulty making ends meet long before your fiscal new year.

A budget should be used for financial planning and better cash management throughout the year. Plan on reviewing your budget at least quarterly, and perhaps monthly. Regular budget reviews should determine how far actual finances have deviated from the budget and why.

Differences between actual and budgeted income and expenses may be due to seasonal expenses, unanticipated expenses, delayed funding, insufficient fund-raising efforts, or an unrealistic budget. At this point, the financial plan must be revised to reflect the real situation. If your original estimates for expenses and/or income are not realistic, adjust them during regular budget reviews. If the budget review indicates an upcoming crunch or deficit, corrective action must be taken to avoid a financial crisis.

The corrective action can include expanding your fund raising and/or cutting back on expenses. The earlier corrective action is taken, the more likely it is that you will be able to avoid cutting back on staff and programs, taking out a loan, and going into debt. Effective use of the budgeting process allows you to catch small problems and alleviate them before the organization finds itself in a financial stranglehold.

HOW DO YOU DEVELOP A BUDGET?

The starting point of any budget is a well-planned program. When you have determined in detail your goals and objectives, outlined your program and methods, and planned your staffing pattern, you are ready to develop a budget.

What kind of a staff do you need, and what should you pay them? What are your space and equipment needs? What will these cost? What about conferences, publications, and other items you feel are necessary to keep the staff informed? How much will it cost to inform the public of your program (to pay for printing, mass mailings, posters, et cetera)?

Fledgling organizations will find it more difficult to project future expenses without the financial records and past experience that older agencies

...g. It is helpful to discuss expenses with, ...imilar to yours.

...ped by the agency's director, but it is im-...nce of the board members, especially the ...process of budget development. Final ap-...sibility of the board of directors as a whole.

...D A BUDGET INCLUDE?

The budget should include all of the anticipated expenditures and income of an organization during a fiscal year. The expenditures include all of the costs of purchasing the services, space, and supplies necessary to operate your program. Income includes all of the projected sources of support: grants, contracts, donations, fees. The fiscal year is a 365-day financial rec-ordkeeping period beginning on the date designated by the board of direc-tors in the organization's bylaws.

A budget includes both fixed and variable costs. Fixed costs are those that remain stable each month, regardless of the level of activity or service. Examples are salaries and rent. Variable costs change directly with the level of use or activity. Postage, printing, and publication costs are variable. Telephone expenses are both fixed and variable. There are monthly charges, which are fixed, and charges for long-distance calls, which vary.

Fixed costs are easier to determine, although you should take into ac-count any anticipated changes during the year: rent increases and salary in-creases, for example. You must estimate variable costs as best you can, but you should remember to include seasonal as well as average monthly costs. For instance, postage estimates should include the cost of stamps and post-age used each month as well as the annual bulk mail permit fee and the cost of the several bulk mailings you may have planned for the coming year.

Be realistic! Don't underestimate your expenses or overestimate your expected income. On the other hand, don't pad, or overestimate, your budget costs either. Be as accurate as you possibly can be.

HOW CAN YOU DETERMINE ANNUAL EXPENSE BUDGET ITEMS?

Personnel

Salaries: The salaries for each regular, paid staff position should be deter-mined separately. These salary figures should reflect employee income before state and federal taxes are withheld. Salary schedules for each position should be developed by calling similar organizations within your community and requesting information on their salary schedules. Salary determination calls for a balance between what your organization can reasonably afford to pay and what you need to pay to attract people with the skills you need to perform your services.

Interns, Typists, and Other Part-time Employees: The amount of money needed to pay part-time help used periodically is more difficult to determine. You must consider the type of tasks to be performed, the amount of time it will take to perform them, and the hourly wages for each type of job. Each job should be calculated separately.

Consultants: Consulting fees cover payments to people providing services directly to the staff, such as trainers, accountants, and evaluators. Fees for an annual financial audit (which could be substantial) should be included here.

Health and Life Insurance: Although optional, health and life insurance are benefits generally provided by employers. Insurance costs depend on the type and amount of coverage purchased and the age and health of each individual covered. Call a couple of reliable insurance agents and ask them for quotes on both health and life insurance. Ask similar organizations about their insurance rates. Estimates for new organizations will be rough.

Unemployment Insurance: A tax may be required of all organizations and businesses within your state to maintain a public state fund for unemployment benefits. Such benefits are based on a percentage of an employee's wages. Call the taxation division in your state to determine the rate of taxation for your organization.

Workers' Compensation: States generally require businesses and organizations to hold insurance policies that will compensate employees for salary lost and expenses incurred from injuries or diseases due to work-related tasks. These insurance rates are regulated by the state, although the policies are purchased through private insurance companies. Call the workers' compensation division of your state's department of labor for information on the regulations and rates that apply to your organization. The rates are related to the amount of health risk that each job entails.

Social Security: Social security (FICA) taxes are optional for nonprofit organizations. However, if an organization chooses to participate in the social security program, all of the employees must be included; contribution is not on an individual basis. If the organization chooses to participate, both the employees and the organization pay into the fund at the same rate.

Staff Development: An organization may choose to make available some funds (sometimes based on a percentage of employee's salaries, perhaps between 1 percent and 5 percent) to be used by employees for further education and training in their fields.

Physical Facility

Rent: If you do not have office space at the time you are developing your budget, it is hard to determine an exact rental figure. You should identify a potential neighborhood and ask a realtor for the going rate, per square feet, for office space in that area. After you have determined the amount of space needed in terms of square feet, you then multiply this by the rate estimate given by the realtor.

If you plan to share a facility with an existing agency, determine the amount of space you will occupy and multiply this by the rate per square foot the agency is paying.

Utilities: Monthly charges on gas, electricity, and water may or may not be included in rent payments. If most of your rent estimates have included utilities, you do not need a separate budget item. However, if they have not, ask potential landlords for estimates of monthly utilities payments.

Telephone: Ask the local phone company for a rate schedule. The rate varies, depending upon the type of system chosen and the number of phones installed. Don't forget to get a quote on the cost of installation and add it to your first year's budget. Also, estimate the cost of anticipated long-distance calls.

Janitorial Services: Many times rental leases do not include this service. Estimates for janitorial services are based on the square footage of your office space. Include this item in your budget if rental estimates have not included janitorial services.

Purchased Equipment: First, list the items needed: desks, chairs, tables, files, typewriters, adding machines, et cetera. If you are just starting out, these costs can be very high. Seek low-cost alternatives to purchasing new equipment, such as donations from corporations of furniture and equipment, and the purchase of used or rebuilt equipment. For anything that you cannot obtain free or at low cost, you should obtain estimates.

Rented Equipment: Instead of purchasing equipment such as typewriters and copying machines, you can rent it on a monthly basis or on longer leases. Call various rental businesses and seek quotes on the items you need. Sometimes rental payments can be applied to the purchase price of the equipment later.

Equipment Maintenance: Machines such as typewriters and copiers require regular maintenance, especially as they get older. If you own such equipment, ask an office equipment dealer about the cost of maintenance contracts.

Other Costs

Supplies: This is a tough one! It is very hard to figure how much in the way of pencils, pens, paper, envelopes, letterhead, typewriter ribbons, staples, tape, et cetera, a specific number of staff members will go through in one year. Again, check with organizations that are of a similar size and have similar functions to see how much they spend. Otherwise, make a list of the items you think will be needed (an experienced office manager can help here) and visit an office supplies store to check their prices.

Postage: There is no simple way to calculate the number of letters you plan to write per year, so just make a stab at it and multiply that number by the going postal rate. If you plan mailings of more than 200 letters, flyers, or newsletters at a time, check into the cost of a bulk mail permit. For such bulk mailings, estimate the number and size of such mailings that you might do in a year and check with the post office for the going rate per piece for bulk mail permit holders (it is much less expensive). There is also an annual bulk mail permit fee, so be sure to include that fee in your budget, also.

Publications/Subscriptions: First, figure out which periodicals (newsletters, magazines, journals) you wish to subscribe to and obtain subscription costs for each. Next, make a list of the books and other written materials (training manuals, directories) you know you want, with their prices. Leave some room in the budget for other materials of which you may not yet be aware. If you are a new organization and plan on developing a library of materials, plan to spread the cost of these materials over two or three years. This can be an expensive endeavor, especially if you try to do it in one chunk.

Service Agreements: This includes things like data processing, bookkeeping services, computer time, and other service contracts that you might need. Again, estimate what will be needed and to what extent and contact the experts for estimates and advice on the amount of service you will need.

Printing and Photocopying: This is another difficult item to estimate! Try to make an educated guess about monthly photocopying needs (for smaller copying jobs) and printing needs (for larger copying jobs). Again, it helps to talk to someone in a similar organization. Watch your costs closely during the first few months of the budget year; you may need to revise this budget item during the year.

Conferences: Attempt to itemize and estimate the fees for conferences and workshops that your staff may attend. It is very hard to anticipate future conferences and costs, but, again, you can talk to those in similar organizations and keep track of your expenditures carefully so you can make a budget adjustment mid-year, if necessary.

Travel: This includes mileage reimbursement, bus fares, and taxi fares. Calculate the number of miles per month each staff person may need to drive for job-related purposes and anticipate the number of bus and taxi trips. Estimate yearly costs on the basis of these figures by using a preset cents-per-mile reimbursement figure.

Advertising: This includes newspaper advertising for staff positions as well as advertising for your program in the community. There are many low-cost ways of advertising your program, so you need not plan on an expensive media campaign before you try other approaches.

Insurance: Your organization may need several kinds of insurance: bonding, theft, fire, vehicle, malpractice, and liability. Talk to an insurance agent (ask the director of another small, nonprofit agency to recommend one) about your needs and the costs of each type of insurance your organization requires.

Fees: Itemize the membership fees and licenses you anticipate for staff members and the organization and obtain estimates of current rates.

Petty Cash: This fund is used for small office expenses. Set it up for a monthly amount and keep close track of petty cash expenses so that adjustments can be made in either your spending or the budget.

HOW TO DETERMINE THE INCOME BUDGET

The second part of the budget outlines anticipated income. An agency rarely has a total commitment for funding for an upcoming year at the time it begins the budgeting process (usually three to six months before the onset of the new budget year). Therefore, it is necessary to estimate as accurately as possible income from those recurring sources upon which you can depend for funds.

If you provide some services for fees, you can begin by estimating how many participants you will serve in each of your programs during the coming year and determining the fee structure you will use. These figures should give you a handle on how much client-generated fee income you can anticipate. Such fees include program service fees, income from the sale of publications or products, and client fees covered by third-party reimbursement, such as insurance payments and county contracts.

Contributions from individuals may also play an important part of your income plan. Funds to be raised from special events and benefits can and should be estimated (remember to include the costs of putting on such events in the budget). Another source of income could be earnings on endowment investments if you have any.

Since these three items and client or membership fees are more in your control than are grants, you must try to be as precise as possible in estimating the income you may derive from these. The balance of your support, depending upon your specific programs, will come from various private or public grants or governmental contracts.

Outline as precisely as possible all the grants and/or contracts you anticipate receiving from outside sources. Be reasonable in your expectations from these sources, taking into account your past experience with the fundor and/or your initial inquiries. This step of budget development is especially difficult for new programs, which have no funding history on which to base projections. At this stage, you should ask those sources you are most sure of to confirm their interest in you and to estimate the amount of their grants.

When the anticipated income from all these sources is added together, the difference between this figure and your expense budget is the amount you still need to raise from undetermined sources. Mostly these will be foundations and corporations you have not previously approached or of whom you are less sure. If this figure is a large portion of your budget, you may have set unrealistically high income goals for yourself, and you should consider either trimming back expenses or beefing up other sources of income.

When your budget-planning committee meets during the months before the beginning of a new fiscal year, you should be prepared to propose prioritized spending decreases or increases from initial budget plans, depending upon the progress you make with your funding sources.

WHICH BUDGET FORMAT SHOULD BE USED?

A budget usually takes one of three formats. The first, and simplest, merely lists expenses according to the areas listed in the previous budget outline. (This is called a *summary budget*.) Expenses are listed in a single column, and the cost of each item is listed as a total. This format is used for the budgets of organizations that are small and/or that have a fairly simple structure, providing only one major program out of one facility.

The second format outlines the organization's expenses according to the service or program areas. (This is called a *functional budget*.) For instance, a community clinic that provides an extensive counseling program and an educational outreach program as well as clinical services may find it most useful to organize its budget in terms of these program areas. This format outlines the costs of providing each of these services. Often, organizations raise funds separately for each program area, and this budget format is essential in these cases.

A functional budget may or may not have a separate column for administrative costs. These are expenses that relate directly to running the overall program and include staff time spent in management, fund raising, bookkeeping, budget reporting, supervision, and other administrative tasks. It is easier to have a separate column for general operating costs and often enlightening to see how much it actually costs to keep the program running. However, it is difficult to raise funds separately for administration, and for proposal purposes you may wish to allocate administrative costs to each of the program areas for which you raise funds.

The third budget format is based on the geographical units of an organization and is used for larger organizations with branch offices. The costs for the budget items are distributed according to office units. If there are expenses that apply to each of the units (such as administrative expenses), these should be distributed among the units according to appropriate proportions.

CASH FLOW: WHERE IS YOUR MONEY WHEN YOU NEED IT?

The budget is a valuable tool in that it tells you how much you expect to spend during a one-year period and how much money you expect to raise during this same period. However, there is another crucial piece of information you need: Will the money be available when you need to spend it?

It is one thing to be able to say that you will raise $45,000 in a year to cover anticipated expenses of $45,000. It is another to have cash in the bank when you have to pay your bills. In order to avoid a money crunch, it is helpful to develop a "cash flow" chart that outlines your anticipated expenses and income on a monthly basis.

The budget worksheet (reproduced at the end of this section) you use while developing your budget can serve as a basis for outlining your cash flow. Although most organizations have fairly steady monthly expenses, they can fluctuate due to several factors: seasonal expenses, raises in salaries or rent, more or fewer staff members during the year, large, one-time-only expenses (furniture, telephone installation, printing brochures), et cetera. You must try to anticipate how your expenses will be distributed monthly during the fiscal year.

You must also estimate when you will receive anticipated income from each of your identified sources: fees, grants, contracts, et cetera. Remember that fund raising takes time and that it will be months between an initial contact date and the actual receipt of money.

Outline your anticipated income and expenses per month at every three months but preferably for a six-month period. If there appears to be a period when you will not have enough money to meet expenses, determine (1) whether it is realistic to anticipate that funds to cover these expenses will be available during a later period in the year, and (2) if so, whether you should cover these expenses with a loan to be repaid when the cash is available (remember the interest rates!) or you can delay some of the expenses (furniture purchases can be delayed, salaries should not be), and, if not, you must determine how to cut back on your expenses.

The cash flow chart should also be used to compare estimated monthly expenses and income with the actual figures. Review your projected and actual cash flow for each quarter. If you have consistently overestimated your expected income or underestimated your expenses, you should examine the reason this happened and consider additional fund-raising efforts or a decreased pattern of spending.

HOW SHOULD THE BUDGET BE REVISED?

Budget planning, especially for new organizations, is a difficult task, and some planning errors are almost inevitable. Nevertheless, changes in the budget during the fiscal year should be made with caution. All budget changes, especially increases in the budget, should be approved by the board of directors. Minor changes that do not result in a budget increase can generally be made without board approval, but these changes should be reported to the board.

It is also important to avoid major changes in your budget so that you can compare your planning of expenditures and income with your actual performance. If the budget is changed every time a problem occurs, there will be no way of measuring how well the executive director and the board planned the budget and were able to use it as a management tool.

SAMPLE BUDGET

Annual Expense Budget

Personnel

Director	$ 18,000
Associate Director	15,000
Counseling Coordinator	14,300
Recreation Specialist (2/3 time)	8,000
Educational Services Coordinator	13,000
Family Counselor (2/3 time)	7,225
Youth Counselor	14,445
Office Coordinator	9,100
Secretary	6,773
Bookkeeper (1/2 time)	5,250
Intern	2,184
Temporary Typist	400
	113,677

Benefits

Health Insurance	3,900
Life Insurance	555
Unemployment	3,100
Workers' Compensation	700
Staff Development	3,350
	11,605

Other Costs

Travel	1,566
Conferences	2,000
Fees/Licenses	300
Publications/Subscriptions	600
Supplies	2,050
Consultants	1,500
Audit	1,000
Rent	7,650
Telephone	3,600
Postage	1,300
Insurance	250
Equipment	1,000
Advertising	1,350
Printing/Copying	800
Janitorial Service	900
Computer Services	600
Equipment Maintenance	200
Petty Cash	360
	27,026

Total	$152,308

SAMPLE BUDGET (Continued)

Budget Explanations

Health Insurance	$35/person/month
Life Insurance	$5/person/month
Unemployment	4%/year
Workers' Compensation	$90,000 at 69¢/$100; $23,000 at 23¢/$100
Staff Development	3% of salaried positions ($111,000)
Travel	Bus: $95; mileage reimbursement: 1,470 miles at 17.5¢/mile
Conferences	Based on 1.8% of salaries
Consultants	10 days/year at $150/day
Rent	6 months at $525/month; 6 months at $750 month
Telephone	$275/month; long distance: $25/month
Equipment	Easel, projector, office furniture
Printing/Copying	500/month at 10¢; plus printing audit and annual report
Janitorial Service	$75/month
Equipment Maintenance	Typewriter service contracts: 2 at $75; $50 miscellaneous maintenance

Income Budget

Service–Generated Income

Client Fees	$22,500
Educational Fees	10,500
County Contract	<u>17,500</u>
	50,500

Anticipated Grants

State Grant	21,620
Juniper Foundation	16,000
Sunrise Foundation	10,000
Brown Corporation	5,000
Energetics, Inc.	3,000
Monroe Foundation	3,000
Stephens Foundation	2,000
Service Club	2,000
Northern Plains Foundation	6,000
Smith & Smith, Inc.	<u>1,000</u>
	69,620

Art Auction	3,500
Funds to Be Raised	28,688

Proposals will be submitted to fifteen local and
state foundations and corporations during the
fiscal year.

Total	$152,308

BUDGET WORKSHEETS

Use this worksheet to compile a rough draft of your budget. The worksheet can be a useful tool throughout the fiscal year because it outlines, not only the total amount needed for each item, but also outlines in detail how you arrived at these totals and provides a basis for the development of a monthly cash flow chart. Project anticipated expenses for one fiscal year for each of these items.

I. *PERSONNEL*

SALARIES

(1) Director: $_____ per month or $_____ annually

(2)

(3)

(4)

(5)

(6)

(7)

(8)

(9)

(10)   _____

                              TOTAL Salaries $

EMPLOYEE BENEFITS

State Unemployment Insurance
    (____% on first $_____/employee) $
Worker's Compensation
FICA/Social Security
    (____% on first $_____/employee)
Health Insurance (average of
    $_____per month/employee
Life Insurance (average of
    $_____ per month/employee)
Staff Development and Training
    (____% of employees' salaries)

                                             _____

                              TOTAL Benefits $
                                                         _____

                    TOTAL—PERSONNEL $

II. *FACILITY*

RENT AND UTILITIES

      Rent ($_____/month) $

      Utilities:

         Gas ($_____/month)

         Electricity ($_____/month)

         Water ($_____/month)

         Other ($_____/month)

                          TOTAL _____ $

TELEPHONE

      Basic Service ($_____/month) $

      Long Distance (average of

         $_____/month)

      Installation

                          TOTAL _____ $

EQUIPMENT

      Desks: #_____ @ $_____ $

      Chairs: #_____ @ $_____

      File Cabinets: #_____ @ $_____

      Bookcases: #_____ @ $_____

      Typewriters: #_____ @ $_____

      Other Office Machines:

      Other Office Furniture:

                          TOTAL _____ $

MAINTENANCE

      Janitorial Service $

         ($_____/month)

      Repair fund (if necessary)

                          TOTAL _____ $

                TOTAL—FACILITY $

III. *OTHER COSTS*

SUPPLIES

Letterhead and Envelopes $
Other Office Supplies

TOTAL _____ $

POSTAGE

Postage (average of $_____/month) $
Annual Fee for Bulk Mail Permit
Bulk Mail Postage Estimate

TOTAL _____ $

PUBLICATIONS AND SUBSCRIPTIONS

Annual Subscription Fees $
Books, Pamphlets, et cetera

TOTAL _____ $

CONFERENCES

Conference and Workshop Fees $

TOTAL _____ $

TRAVEL

Local Travel Reimbursement
  (average of $_____/month) $
Out-of-Town Travel

TOTAL _____ $

PRINTING AND COPYING

Copying ($_____/month) $
Printing ($_____/month)
Printing of Brochures
Other Printing for Special Jobs

TOTAL _____ $

CONSULTANTS

Auditing and/or Accounting $
Legal Services
Public Relations/Brochure Design

BUDGET WORKSHEET (Continued)

CONSULTANTS (Continued) $
    Evaluation Consultation
    Other

             TOTAL   _____ $

INSURANCE

    Liability $
    Vehicle
    Other

             TOTAL   _____ $

FEES

    Incorporation $
    Registration with State
    Membership Fees for
      Professional or Service Affiliations
    Other

             TOTAL   _____ $ _____

           TOTAL—OTHER COSTS $

_____-_____ FISCAL YEAR TOTAL EXPENSES $

EXPECTED INCOME

	SOURCE	MONTH OF RECEIPT OR $____/MONTH	AMOUNT
Foundation Grants (list if you have specific commitments):			
Government Grants (list specific grant program):			
Government Contracts (list specific sources: state, county, city, federal):			
Individual Contributions:			
Special Events:			
Income from Client Fees:			
Other:			

           TOTAL EXPECTED INCOME $

Fund Raising:
Finding the $$$$

Fund raising is the nitty-gritty problem of your nonprofit organization. Where does the money come from? Who will fund your program? How can you develop a funding strategy to keep your organization operating effectively?

The size of this chapter does not begin to reflect the enormity of the task of raising funds for an organization. However, the weight of the bibliography following the chapter is an indication of the wealth of valuable books and other materials available in the area of grantsmanship. Instead of duplicating information accessible in some excellent resources, this chapter provides an introduction to funding sources and proposal writing. Depending on which type of funding source best meets your needs, you can choose relevant resources from the bibliography to get more detailed information on how best to approach your sources of funds.

Most of the reference books listed at the end of this chapter are available in the Foundation Center Regional Collections located in fifty-six libraries throughout the United States, Puerto Rico, and Mexico. The Regional Collections are small reference libraries with materials about foundations and foundation grants, government grants, proposal writing, and fund raising. They are a useful starting point for funding research.

The centers are a project of the Foundation Center, a nonprofit organization founded in 1956 to gather, analyze, and disseminate information about philanthropic foundations. To locate the Foundation Center Regional Collection nearest you, you can contact the Foundation Center, 888 Seventh Avenue, New York, N.Y. 10019 (212-975-1120). In Minnesota, there is a regional collection in the sociology department of the Central Minneapolis Library. There, a trained staff can show the public how to use the collection.

Fund raising and grantsmanship are skills crucial to the nonprofit organization. Generally, both the board of directors and the director of the organization are active in this area. It is not necessary for the small nonprofit organization to seek out the expertise of a professional fund raiser. Many of the most successful fund raisers learned the fine art of grantsmanship as they struggled to find funds for their fledgling programs. With time and energy invested in basic research, anyone should be able to understand the basics of grantsmanship.

FUNDING SOURCES

Private Funding Sources

Family Foundations: Generally, these foundations were established by wealthy individuals or families to fund charitable programs according to the donors' wishes. Local institutions and causes favored by the donors are the major beneficiaries. These foundations usually are governed by family members, and most do not have full-time staffs. Many are staffed by outside professionals working on a part-time basis. Large family foundations, however, usually employ a full-time staff. The three largest family foundations in Minnesota are the Bush Foundation, the McKnight Foundation, and Northwest Area Foundation.

Corporate Foundations: Corporate foundations are set up by business corporations to facilitate the disbursement of charitable contributions. Although legally independent of the sponsoring company, the corporate foundation is generally governed by trustees who are also company officers. A corporate foundation often focuses its contributions in communities where the corporation operates and in service areas of interest to the corporation or its employees.

Most corporate foundations give amounts equal to less than 1 percent of the corporation's income before taxes, although as much as 5 percent is legally tax deductible. Examples of corporate foundations in Minnesota are those of Honeywell, Minnesota Mining and Manufacturing, and General Mills.

Some corporations and smaller businesses do not form separate foundations but instead donate funds directly. Generally, funds granted from these businesses are more limited and go to projects more directly related to the interests of the company or its owner.

Community Foundations: These are professionally staffed foundations that receive money from many local sources (smaller family foundations, gifts, and estates) and distribute it to local causes according to the instructions of the donors. One staff, then, does the work for many funding sources and small foundations. Community foundations are governed by a board of prominent local citizens.

Although most of the funds handled by community foundations are designated for specific beneficiaries or service areas, there are some open-ended and unrestricted funds available for other causes. A wide variety of programs are supported by community foundations due to the broad range of their donors' interests. The oldest community foundations are the Minneapolis Foundation and the Cleveland Foundation.

General Purpose Foundations: General purpose, or independent, foundations are those four hundred or so large, well-endowed foundations that are national in scope. They have large, full-time staffs and prestigious boards of directors. Although most were established by extremely wealthy families or individuals, the foundations are usually not closely influenced by their donors or the donors' families. In general, they give large grants to special and innovative projects that may have far-reaching impact. The Ford Foundation, the Rockefeller Foundation, and the Carnegie Foundation are examples of this type of foundation. Despite the large scope of these foundations, small local organizations are not necessarily excluded from consideration for grants.

Special Purpose Foundations: These foundations were established usually through a will or a trust, to give money to one specific cause—a scholarship fund or a specific college, for example. Although these foundations follow very restrictive guidelines, exceptions are sometimes made and grants are given to programs outside the foundations' usual areas.

Service Clubs and Churches: Membership organizations—civic clubs (Kiwanis, Lions), fraternal organizations (Elk, Moose), and women's clubs—also donate funds to projects of interest to them. The proposal process is less formal and more personal. Generally, such organizations give small amounts to local community and neighborhood projects. Religious groups —including neighborhood, city-wide, and national units of churches—can also be important sources of funding.

United Way: United Way or United Fund organizations annually conduct a centralized fund-raising campaign among individuals, businesses, and foundations and disburse these funds to member agencies. Although usually affiliated with the national United Way, each community United Way organization functions autonomously. There are over four hundred affiliated united or community funds just in the state of Minnesota. United Way tends to support well-established, "traditional" agencies such as scouting groups, multiservice centers, and services for senior citizens and the handicapped.

Larger United Way organizations have full-time, professional staffs and are governed by a board of directors composed of community members. In addition to fund raising, larger United Way units also provide planning and coordination for member agencies. In addition, there has been a recent move among some units to provide expanded management support and program evaluation to member agencies.

Generally, the application process for consideration for United Way funding must begin about a year before the next funding period, according to the fiscal and decision-making timetable of each United Way organization. Although new agencies may apply for United Way membership, only a small amount of United Way funding is given to agencies and programs in their early stages of development, unless they are affiliated with current United Way organizations. In most cases, approval for membership implies ongoing United Way support, although budget requests for each program are reviewed annually.

Public Funding Sources

On the other side of the coin is government funding. A growing number of private, nonprofit agencies receive some or all of their money from one or more government units. Government funding is available from units at several levels—federal, state, county, and city. The new "federalism" manifested by the recent move to increased revenue sharing returned much of the decision-making responsibility regarding local grants to state and local units of government.

Public funding differs significantly from private funding in the proposal process, accountability requirements, and guideline compliance in such areas as hiring practices. Public funding takes one of several forms.

Grants: Grants are funds awarded by a government unit to private institutions or state or local units of government for the support of programs originated and defined by the agencies themselves. Project grants provide funds for service delivery, research, training, technical assistance, facilities, and equipment.

Contracts: Funds are awarded by a government unit to public or private agencies through contracts, which are legal agreements, to purchase assistance in carrying out its own program goals. Such assistance can include surveys and studies, evaluation services, consulting, training, conferences, and production of publications and other materials.

Request for Proposal, or RFP: A request for proposal issued by a government unit solicits proposals for a grant or a contract for a specific service or activity outlined by the RFP.

Purchase of Service: A governmental agency, rather than delivering services directly with its own employees, may provide for delivery by contracting with private agencies to provide these services. The government unit, in effect, buys services for its clients from private agencies through purchase of service agreements.

Conclusion: It may be harder to find out the most appropriate public funding source from which to seek support than it is to choose which private resources to approach. Maintaining informal contacts and keeping up-to-date on funding activities related to your field are especially important. In addition, you should

1.   find out which local and state government units relate to your service area. If they issue newsletters, you should be sure to receive them.
2.   know and contact legislators (both state and federal) on key related committees.
3.   identify and attend conferences in your field (local, regional, and, if possible, national). The contacts you make there can be invaluable.
4.   talk to others from similar programs who have recently received public funding.

Fees for Service

This type of funding is more appropriate for some types of programs than for others, depending on the clients involved and the services offered. In some cases, third-party fee payment is possible. For instance, payment for chemical dependency treatment is generally covered by the medical insurance of the client. Other programs charge fees according to a sliding fee scale based on the client's income and ability to pay. Sales of publications produced by an organization are also considered as fees for service. Membership organizations receive income from membership fees. Fees for service usually constitute only a small portion of a nonprofit organization's projected income, however, because of the objective of providing services to those who need them, regardless of their ability to pay. Nevertheless, private and public funding sources often want the programs they support to charge fees, however small, to those clients who can afford them.

PROPOSAL DEVELOPMENT

Proposal Planning

The first step in looking for funding is a simple one: make sure that the program you are proposing is worth funding. You must have, not just a worthwhile idea, but a well-planned and carefully defined program. Potential fundors must be able to get a clear understanding of what it is you are asking them to support.

Throughout the early planning stage, write down key points and ideas that may be useful during proposal writing. Proposals should be written only after the purpose and scope of the program have been carefully delineated, its relationship to existing community resources outlined, methods and target population defined.

During the planning stage, you also should gather documentation of the needs that your program proposes to meet. Such documentation should include demographic and census data related to your service area that give basic information about your target population (age, education, income, et cetera) and the extent of the problems you are addressing (rates of drug abuse, unemployment and crime, extent of deteriorated housing, degree of environmental damage, et cetera). Such data are available from state, county, and city departments in the areas of health, welfare, crime and delinquency, planning, recreation, and law enforcement. Private agencies that serve the same target population you will also should be able to give you information in these areas. Any studies and reports, especially local ones, that are related to your program area may also provide documentation.

In addition, outline the services currently available to your potential constituency. What services will you provide that differ from those already available? How will your program interact with these? Your program will not be viewed in isolation; it will be considered as part of a network of services and programs. You must be able to explain where your organization will fit into that network.

Contact other persons involved in your field, especially those from agencies your program will be working with, receiving referrals from, and making referrals to. Other support and input should be solicited from related bodies or from legislators. Get this input early in the planning process and identify those people who support your proposed program and are willing to serve as references for potential fundors. Solicit letters of support from such contacts.

Following these steps is necessary to persuade fundors that your proposal is necessary and worthwhile and to ensure that you develop a program that will be effective and responsive to the needs of those you serve. If you cannot persuade any fundors that your program is worthwhile, it may not be!

Identifying Potential Funding Sources

The directories and other resources described in the bibliography at the end of this chapter can be used to develop a list of possible fundors for your program. You should contact others from similar or related programs to ask them about their funding sources and about others they are aware of.

First, identify the sources that seem like possibilities. Is your program in their interest area? Have they funded similar programs? Do your funding needs fit within the range of their average grant size? Is the timing of their grant-making process favorable (or will you just miss a once-a-year deadline)? Next, narrow your list to several likely possibilities. For each of these sources, find out (1) the application procedures and deadlines; (2) the reporting requirements, if funded; (3) how granting decisions are made and by whom; and (4) whether you could develop a good working relationship with this funding source. If this information is not available from outside sources, contact the funding source itself.

It is important to consider the side effects of funding from some sources. Occasionally, fundors try to exert control over your program and require changes. Some (government funding units, in particular) require extensive reporting and conformity to specific guidelines. Those side-effects can require much time and some compromise on your part. Your group must decide whether the requirements of a particular funding source are acceptable to you.

At this point, you should have a few sources on which to focus your initial funding research. Write each source a letter outlining your program (form letters should never be used!), explaining who you are, what you plan to do, how you will do it, and how much it will cost, and asking whether they are interested in seeing a complete proposal for your program. If you can arrange it, a personal meeting with the funding source could take the place of this initial letter. If not, follow up your letter with a telephone call to request a face-to-face meeting.

This initial contact is important. It can save time and money if you avoid sending proposals to funding sources that are not interested or for which you do not qualify.

If the funding source is interested, elicit advice about your proposal's content, format, and length and any other suggestions that may improve your chances of obtaining funding.

Developing and Submitting Proposals

Some of the places to which you will send proposals (government agencies, in particular) will have application forms that must be completed. Others merely outline broadly what the proposal should include. Be sure to obtain the most recent proposal guidelines and forms for application. In either case, you should develop a proposal that should include the following sections.

Overview: Briefly summarize your program, who you are, what you propose to do, and how much money you need. This should be a cover page and can be in the form of a cover letter. The summary is important because it is the first thing the funding source will read and it may be used during an initial screening process.

Organization's Qualifications: In the body of the proposal, describe the background and history of your organization, your community support, and the past accomplishments of your organization or of your staff and board members. The proposal should explain how the organization got started and why. Letters of support from key community members and representatives of other agencies can be included in an appendix. Copies of any newspaper articles about your program or those involved in it can also be included.

Problem or Need: Document the problem: the existing conditions, their scope, and their impact on the community. You should refer to important statistics, related reports, surveys, and assessments of the problem by community representatives and professionals in the field. The problem should be defined in terms of what your program can realistically address. If the problem appears too overwhelming to fundors, they will feel that your program and the money they put into it would never be able to have an impact on the problem. You should be specific as to what you think your impact on the problem will be.

Goals and Objectives: Your proposal should describe the intended outcomes of your program and its effect on the problem you have described. Again, you must be realistic. Your objectives should be achievable. They should also be measurable, and they should refer to the changes that will be brought about through your program. The goals and objectives should follow directly from your definition of the problem. You must not confuse methods with objectives.

Methods: Objectives speak about outcomes; methods describe the process used to reach the objectives. Outline the activities you will conduct to accomplish your objectives, including a timetable, if possible. You should include your rationale for using these methods instead of others.

Staff: Your proposal should include a description of the responsibilities and qualifications of the program's staff; it should outline the structure of the organization (organizational chart of decision-making processes), also.

Evaluation: Describe how you will measure your program's effectiveness and whether or not you have achieved your goals and objectives. Indicate whether this evaluation process will be in-house or whether you will use an outside consultant.

Future Funding: If the funding source is not being asked to fund the entire program, where will the rest of the funding come from? Outline plans for funding, present and future. Fundors look for a well-planned funding strategy that indicates that you are not permanently or totally dependent upon them and that you have thought out your funding future realistically.

Budget: The proposal should list proposed expenditures, including salaries and benefits, rent, utilities, equipment, supplies, et cetera. It should also outline projected income. The budget should be realistic. Are you trying to run a $100,000 program on a $50,000 budget? Or are you asking for $100,000 for a program that could be conducted for $50,000? If your objectives and methods somehow do not match the scope of your budget, your credibility could be damaged.

Appendix: Copies of your letters of support, staff résumés, list of board members, letter of tax exemption, and any statistical charts and newspaper clippings about your organization can be attached to your proposal as an appendix.

Most of the information to be included in your proposal should have been gathered during your early planning stages. After the proposal has been written, test it out on someone else—a few concerned (and frank) critics who will read the proposal and offer suggestions. (The chapters on program planning and budget development will be helpful for proposal planning, too.)

Proposals should be typed or printed and accompanied by a personal cover letter addressed to the director of the funding source. It is acceptable to submit identical proposals to a number of fundors at the same time. Each proposal, however, should ask for a specific amount of money. You should not ask each fundor for the total amount needed. Most fundors do not wish to be your sole source of support.

The cover letter should indicate any other sources from which you are seeking funds, any sources who have supported you in the past, and long-range funding plans. (Most sources do not want to fund you forever!)

The size of a proposal should generally be related to the amount of money requested. Don't submit a twenty-five page proposal for a $3,000 budget! Smaller grant requests need only short proposals, although most of the areas outlined should be briefly addressed.

Follow-up

You should call a week or two after you submitted the proposal if you have not heard from the agency or foundation. Ask if you can set up a meeting. Personal contact at this point is critical. The decision-making process is a lengthy one. It is legitimate to keep in touch to see how things are progressing, but don't hound them.

If funds are not granted, ask the fundors to explain their reasons for rejecting your proposals, and, if it is appropriate, ask whether you could resubmit your proposal at a different point in your development.

If you receive a grant, find out what reporting procedures you should follow. In some cases, periodic progress reports are required. Otherwise, reporting is usually left to your discretion. You should be prepared to give your funding sources information about program activities (especially any major changes in the program), expenditures, staff changes, and any other relevant data. Even if it is not specifically required by funding sources, send your program's annual reports to all your fundors. It is important to develop good ongoing relationships with your fundors. They can be an important source for ideas regarding program development, future funding, and community support. In addition, they can be used as references about your program by other funding sources in the future.

QUESTIONS FUNDORS ASK, OR
"TO SEE YOURSELF AS OTHERS SEE YOU"

After you have completed your proposal, place yourself on the other side of the table by reviewing your proposal through the eyes of your potential fundor, keeping in mind the degree of familiarity with your field that a particular funding source is likely to have.

The rest of the chapter is made up of a list of some of the critical questions that fundors are likely to ask when reviewing proposals.

Has the Program Been Clearly Defined?

Does the proposal clearly describe the purpose, goals, and methods of the program? The reader should be able to tell exactly what the program intends to do and how, with whom, where, when, and why. Someone who is not closely involved in the field should be able to understand your proposal. (You must beware of jargon and define your terms.)

Does the Program Fulfill a Need in the Community?

Include documented analysis of your assessment of the needs of your target population for the services you will provide and the extent to which your program will respond to these needs. Indicate how you assessed these needs—through a survey, research, et cetera. Can the funding source be sure that the needs cited are real?

Does this Program Duplicate Services Offered Elsewhere?

Show that you are aware of other organizations that are working in your problem area and have coordinated your program with theirs. Your referral and resource network should be outlined. If you are duplicating services provided by others in order to demonstrate alternative methods or strategies, explain the differences in your approach to the problem.

Has the Credibiltiy of Your Agency Been Established?

This is a highly subjective judgment on the part of the fundor. One measurement of reliability is your track record—how has your program performed in the past? What other efforts have you (the organization, staff, board members) been involved with? Who in the community supports your project? Your proposal should include letters of support from others in the field and indicate any previous funding sources.

Who's Involved in the Program?

This is closely related to your credibility. Who are your staff members and board of directors? They should be identified, and the ability of the staff to carry out the program and of the board to direct responsibly the organization and raise funds necessary for ongoing support should be documented. The staff's résumés or descriptions of job qualifications should be attached to the proposal.

Is the Proposed Budget Realistic?

Does your budget provide funds sufficient to accomplish your program's objectives (by attracting qualified staff, providing sufficient equipment, et cetera) and yet reflect your cost consciousness?

Where Else Are You Seeking Funds?

Most fundors are reluctant to be a sole source of support for a nonprofit. Your proposal should indicate who else you are approaching, demonstrating your attempt to involve a range of funding sources. Will the contribution of this fundor stimulate giving by others?

What Are Your Future Funding Plans?

If your project is to be ongoing, how will the program be maintained when currently requested funds run out? Most fundors (especially foundations) don't want you leaning on their shoulders too long. If you don't have confirmed plans, you should at least indicate that you have been contacting possible sources for future funding. Discuss the possibility of charging fees for your services.

What Changes Will Your Program Make in Your Clients?
In Your Community?

Have you developed specific, measurable objectives? Clearly describe, in quantitative terms, the changes you want to facilitate in your clients and in the community. Make sure that these projected outcomes are realistic. You must have measurable objectives in order to judge the effectiveness of your program.

How Will You Know Whether You Have Accomplished Your Objectives?

The criteria you plan to use to monitor your progress should be described in your proposal. Develop an evaluation plan. Will the evaluation be internal or involve outside consultants? What instruments and forms, if any, will you use? An evaluation plan will not only give your fundors a means of judging your effectiveness, but more important, it will allow you to refine and improve your program as it develops.

Bibliography

Fund Raising and Proposal Writing

About Foundations: How to Find the Facts You Need to Get a Grant. By Judith Margolin. The Foundation Center, 888 7th Avenue, New York, N.Y. 10019, 1977. Guide for conducting research on foundation funding. Describes material available in the Foundation Center's national and regional collections. Explains how to use foundation annual reports and Internal Revenue Service information returns. (48 pages)

The Art of Winning Foundation Grants. By Howard Hillman and Karin Abarbanel. New York: Vanguard Press, 1975. Basic guide to foundation research: how to find the "right" foundations, how to approach them, how to write a proposal. Describes research tools and sources. Includes sample proposal. (188 pages)

The Art of Winning Government Grants. By Howard Hillman. New York: Vanguard Press, 1977. Outlines federal, state, and local government agencies and how to find out about money available from these sources, how to apply for funding, and what happens to your application. (246 pages)

The Bread Game. By Herb Allen. Glide Publications, 330 Ellis Street, San Francisco, Cal. 94102, 1974. Good basic introduction to fund raising from foundations for the very new agency. Brief introduction to proposal writing, incorporation, accounting, and grant reporting. Sample proposals included. (96 pages)

Developing Skills in Proposal Writing. By Mary Hall. Continuing Education Publications, P.O. Box 1491, Portland, Ore. 97207, 1977. Detailed guide to fund raising from both private and public sources, including idea development, identification of possible fundors, proposal writing. Excellent tool for program planning since it includes a good explanation of needs statements, goals and objectives, evaluation plans, and budgets. Includes sample forms and a good bibliography. (340 pages)

Grants: How to Find Out about Them and What to Do Next. By V. White. Plenum Press, 277 W. 17th Street, New York, N.Y. 10011, 1975. Provides historical and current perspectives on foundation, corporate, and federal grant programs, and covers proposal writing. (354 pages)

The Grass Roots Fund-Raising Book: How to Raise Money in Your Community. By Joan Flanagan. Chicago: Swallow Press, 1977. Guide to putting on local fund-raising events, including such areas as publicity, taxes, and accounting. (219 pages)

Handbook of Special Events for Nonprofit Organizations. By E. Leibert and B. Sheldon. New York: Association Press, 1972. Guide for organizing special fund-raising events, such as art exhibits, fairs, and theater benefits. Topics include idea development, sponsorship, promotion, and reports of example events. (224 pages)

How to Get Government Grants. By Philip Des Marais. Public Service Materials Center, 355 Lexington, New York, N.Y. 10017, 1975. Discusses government grants and contracts, application procedures, and grant reporting, and outlines some of the major federal funding units. Three case studies are included. (155 pages)

How to Raise Money for Kids. Coalition for Children and Youth, 815 15th Street N.W., Washington, D.C. 20005, 1978. Discusses proposal writing, foundation funding, and federal funding. Includes a guide for using the *Catalog of Federal Domestic Assistance* and an extensive bibliography on private and public fund raising. Useful for other programs, too. (50 pages)

Local Fund Development: A Basic Manual for Volunteer Programs. National Center for Voluntary Action, 1214 16th Street N.W., Washington, D.C. 20036, 1974. Focuses on local fund development for relatively low budget volunteer programs. Discusses role of the board in fund raising, budgets, identifying funding sources, and approaching fundors. (44 pages)

The New How to Raise Funds from Foundations. By Joseph Dermer. Public Service Materials Center, 355 Lexington Avenue, New York, N.Y. 10017, 1975. Guide to foundations—their history and current trends, where to find out about foundations, writing the proposal and having the interview, involving "contact." (92 pages)

Stalking the Large Green Grant. National Youth Alternatives Project, 1346 Connecticut, Washington, D.C. 20036, 1976. A fund-raising manual for youth-serving agencies. Outlines possible funding sources, with emphasis on federal government programs. Examples of successful fund raising by youth programs. (72 pages)

Foundation Information

Forms 990-AR and 990-PF are Internal Revenue Service tax returns that describe the grant-making activities of private foundations. These forms are especially helpful in researching smaller foundations that may be excluded from directories. Available on microfiche at Foundation Center Regional Collections.

The Foundation Directory. Columbia University Press, 136 South Broadway, Irvington, N.Y. 10553. Revised periodically. Directory of about 3,000 of the largest foundations in the United States (those granting over $100,000 per year), listed by state and indexed by name, location, and field of interest. Information includes addresses, interest areas, assets, grant sizes, officers of the foundations, and application procedures.

The Foundation Grants Index. Columbia University Press, 136 South Broadway, Irvington, N.Y. 10533. Annual editions. Lists about 10,000 grants awarded during the previous year by about 300 of the largest United States foundations. A compilation of the grants index contained in the bimonthly journal *Foundation News.*

Guide to Minnesota Foundations. Minnesota Council of Foundations, 821 Marquette, Minneapolis, Minn. 55402, 1977. Revision planned for 1980. Lists all Minnesota foundations; for eighty-eight of these, describes their fiscal data and areas of funding interest. Includes general information on Minnesota foundations, their kind, their size, and their grants processes.

Minnesota Foundation Directory. By Beatrice and Frank Capriotti, 123 E. Grant, Minneapolis, Minn. 55403. A detailed listing of all Minnesota foundations, including principal contributors, interest areas, assets, and grants given for the most recent reporting year. Provides a close look at fifty of these foundations, including historical and current perspectives, proposal guidelines, type of initial contact preferred, proper contact person, best time to apply. Loose-leaf format. Updated on annual subscription basis. ($250 initial fee, $150 annual subscription.)

Government Funding Information

The Catalog of Federal Domestic Assistance. United States Government Printing Office, Washington, D.C. 20402. Describes financial and technical resources available through federal funding by over 1,000 different programs. Contains information on grants available, eligibility factors, application procedures, local contacts, et cetera. Loose-leaf in binder. Sold on subscription basis, providing periodic updates.

Commerce Business Daily. United States Government Printing Office, Washington, D.C. 20402. A daily listing of all current potential contracts with the federal government, divided into sections by types of service. (Expensive: $75 per year.)

The Federal Register. United States Government Printing Office, Washington, D.C. 20402. Daily official government periodical. The most current source of information on new and proposed government agency rules and regulations. Includes information on available grants and contracts. However, it is time consuming to plow through and is expensive (about $50 per year, $5 per month). Check a local library.

Minnesota Guidebook to State Agency Services. Office of the State Register, 408 St. Peter, St. Paul, Minn. 55102. Describes all of the departments, boards, and offices of the state government of Minnesota. Includes information on services, grants, reports, licenses. Thorough subject-matter index makes directory easy to use. Revised annually.

United States Government Organization Manual. United States Government Printing Office, Washington, D.C. 20402. The official handbook of the federal government. Describes units and departments of the legislative, judicial, and executive branches, and of certain boards, commissions, and committees. Published annually.

Grantsmanship Journals

Foundation News. Bimonthly magazine published by Council on Foundations, 888 7th Avenue, New York, N.Y. 10019. Includes articles on foundation grant making, administration, and proposal writing. Also includes the foundation grants index, listing recent foundation grants of $5,000 or more by state. ($20 per year.)

Grantsmanship Center News. Bimonthly journal published by the Grantsmanship Center, 1015 W. Olympic Boulevard, Los Angeles, Cal. 90015. Includes articles about developments in public and private funding, planning programs, writing proposals, managing nonprofit programs, and fund raising. ($15 per year.)

Accounting:
Keeping Track of the $$$$

Fledgling organizations need a workable system for recording what they do with their money—keeping track of where it comes from and where it goes. On the other hand, young, nonprofit agencies are often staffed by those unfamiliar with basic accounting methods. If this is the case in your organization, it is important that those who manage the program understand bookkeeping basics and terminology. The purpose of this chapter is to introduce you to the types of records your agency might need, to familiarize you with the elementary components of a bookkeeping system, to define common accounting terms, and to direct you to more comprehensive guides to accounting and bookkeeping.

SETTING UP AN ACCOUNTING SYSTEM

First of all, try to commandeer the services of a willing and able accountant, who can help you set up your bookkeeping system, train you how to use it, and advise you about the most appropriate type of financial reporting for your organization. Board members, professional accounting associations, and business schools may be able to help you find a volunteer accountant. (The search may not be easy, but it certainly helps to have some professional "hand holding" at this stage of the accounting game!)

After you have the "books," you will need a bookkeeper. Very small, volunteer organizations depend on the treasurer of the board of directors to fulfill this role. Small staffed organizations often rely on a paid secretary to do the bookkeeping. Larger agencies sometimes hire a part-time bookkeeper.

A good bookkeeping system provides the means for documenting, recording, summarizing, and reporting the financial transactions of your organization. A written record of your financial history is another benefit. Ultimately, you and your board can use accounting information to make sound financial decisions and to aid in future planning for your organization. The specific information that you get from a good bookkeeping system will:

1. Help you understand how your funds have been used in the past.
2. Help you plan future budgeting and fund-raising needs.
3. Protect your organization against the misuse of funds.
4. Save money by identifying wasteful or inefficient spending.
5. Provide the basis for determining the cost effectiveness of each of your programs.

Demands are placed upon an organization's administrators to provide detailed, accurate cost information about the services they provide. Fundors, governmental bodies, clients, and consumer groups will ask for this information, and you must have the means of providing it. The future of your program may depend on the quality of the financial information you can provide. The board of directors is responsible for ensuring that such information is available.

Many of the basic bookkeeping procedures commonly used by nonprofit organizations are similar to those used by commercial enterprises. Nonprofit organizations are also required to follow other procedures that are unique to their type of operation and sources of income.

CASH- AND ACCRUAL-BASIS ACCOUNTING

One decision both profit and nonprofit organizations must make is whether to keep their financial records on a cash-basis or on an accrual-basis bookkeeping system. In a cash-basis system, financial transactions are recorded at the time they occur. Income is recorded when it is received, and expenses are recorded when they are paid. A cash-basis system accounts for the flow of actual cash through your organization. In an accrual system, however, income is recorded when it is earned, which may be several months before it is actually received, and expenses are recorded when they are incurred, which may be before they are actually paid.

In general, information provided by an accrual bookkeeping system is more useful to an organization because it provides a total financial picture for a given period. Seeing both the amounts due to the organization and the amounts it owes to others, an observer has more information on which to base a financial assessment and to use in making financial projections. However, accrual bookkeeping is more complicated and involves more time-consuming procedures than cash-basis bookkeeping does. This makes it disadvantageous for many small organizations. An alternative many small nonprofits take is to keep their books on a cash-basis system and make accrual adjustments on their financial reports that show amounts due to them and amounts they owe others at the end of the period on which they are reporting.

FUND ACCOUNTING

In fund accounting the specific funds an organization uses for its various purposes are treated separately. The most clear example is money donated to you by an individual or fundor who restricts the use of the funds for specific purposes. Such funds are usually referred to as *restricted funds*, as opposed to *unrestricted funds*, which can be used for the agency's general operations. Some government grantors go so far as to require that their restricted funds be kept in a separate bank account and not be mixed with other monies coming into an agency. In dealing with restricted funds, you should always ask the donor whether it is allowable for you to use those funds for other funds in your program, on a temporary basis, to meet immediate cash needs. Many donors do not permit this.

Another fund that might need to be accounted for on your books is the *plant, building, and equipment fund*. Recorded here are transactions for purchasing buildings or property and all the equipment that has a usable life of over one year and a value of over $100. (Four chairs for your conference table costing $30 apiece would be looked at as a single unit and recorded in this fund.)

The fourth commonly used fund is the *endowment fund*. An endowment is usually a large gift given to you by a person who requires that the principal, or amount of the gift, be kept intact for a given number of years and invested. It is usually provided that any income from an endowment may be used for any purpose designated by the organization's board of directors. For example, John Brown left $50,000 to your organization in his will, provided that none of that money be used for twenty years. Your board invested the money at 8 percent interest and designated that each year the $4,000 interest be used to meet the agency's general operating needs. This then appears as $4,000 income in your unrestricted fund and the balance in your endowment fund remains at $50,000 at the end of each year. Fund accounting, then, allows the observer to look at your funds by the purpose for which they are given to you or have been used by you and alleviates questions about how you have handled specific gifts.

ACCOUNTING FOR DONATED SERVICES AND MATERIALS

Nonprofit agencies depend very heavily on time donated by volunteers and donated supplies and equipment. In many instances, an organization could not carry out its operations without these "in-kind" contributions. It is important, therefore, that such contributions be accounted for by your agency in order to provide a total picture of the costs of your services.

As a rule of thumb, you should include in your financial records and reports those items for which you would have to pay and without which you would be unable to function. Common examples are donated office space, use of another organization's printing and copying machines, volunteer time working with your clients or providing your agency's services, or travel costs or conference costs picked up by employees because there are insufficient funds in your budget to meet them.

In order to count these materials and services as contributions and then as expenses in your program, you must do three things: (1) be able to document that you did receive them, (2) assign a realistic value to them, and (3) have total control over them once they are donated to you. Accounts of donated material and services not only show the total costs of your program, they also provide excellent public relations tools. Such figures show fundors the interest in your organization others have expressed through a donation of time and materials.

Incidentally, volunteer fund-raising efforts usually are not recorded since they do not directly fulfill the organization's objectives or provide services to clients.

FUNCTIONAL OR PROGRAM ACCOUNTING

This is a bookkeeping/accounting method by which costs are assigned to each of the programs an agency may run and to its management and fund-raising functions. Program accounting is designed to answer the question: How much does it cost to operate program A and program B and how much does it cost to manage this agency? Accounting for each program's costs separately helps you present a total, accurate financial picture of your organization and determine the "unit cost" of each program, such as the cost of serving each client or the cost of one hour's service.

Such information allows you to compare the cost of your program to a similar one in the community, and it allows you to see what the results of your fund-raising efforts are in relationship to their costs. It also allows for better budget control and planning for future needs.

Increasingly, fundors, governmental bodies, and various auditing agents are requiring that organizations they audit follow program accounting methods. Assigning costs in such a manner requires carefully followed procedures and detailed recordkeeping: maintaining detailed time records for employees, having purchases authorized by program supervisors so that the bookkeepers know how to charge the costs when checks are written, and determining how office space is actually used by your program. Many costs are then allocated on the basis of percentage of time spent or space used in a given function.

Detailed, consistent recordkeeping by all employees is essential if you are to account for the costs of each of your programs. In general, staff persons resist preparing the detailed paperwork outlined above, and the agency administrator must be able to explain the importance of such cost analysis as an aid to providing better and more effective services to the agency's constituency.

THE BOOKKEEPING SYSTEM

It was stated earlier in the chapter that bookkeeping procedures provide a means of documenting, recording, summarizing, and reporting your financial transactions. This section will address, very briefly, the basic components of a simple cash-basis bookkeeping system. In this type of system, you record the cash income you receive and the disbursement of this cash through checks.

Financial transactions, including cash receipts and cash disbursements, are recorded in chronological order in books called *journals*. Several types of journals may be kept by an organization, depending on the type of information that is to be recorded. All cash and checks received are entered in the *cash receipts journal* in columns with various headings under which you can record the item according to which type of income it is. All checks that you write from your operating account are entered in the *cash disbursements journal* under appropriate expense categories.

Your cash receipts journal should be used to back up the information that appears on your regular bank deposit statements. Bank deposits should be made regularly, preferably daily. Deposit slips should be made in duplicate, with a copy kept to assist in reconciling the bank account at the end of each month and for verification against the cash receipts journals.

It is important that all cash receipts be documented. A numbered receipt should be issued for all cash received, a thankyou letter should be sent for all donations and a copy of it filed, and the voucher or stub of all checks received should be kept to document your deposits.

Also, your agency should get an endorsement stamp from the bank so that you can immediately endorse all checks when they are received in the mail. The endorsement stamp should read "For Deposit Only to the Account of (your organization's name)" and list the bank account number and the name of the bank. This protects you against theft or misuse of funds. Even in the smallest organizations, it is recommended that cash and checks be received and the mail opened by someone other than the person who makes the deposits. A separate list of all the checks and cash received should be kept by this person on a daily basis, and a copy of the list should be passed on to the bookkeeper. This control mechanism is very important, but it is all too often overlooked in agencies that feel they do not have sufficient staff.

Your cash disbursements journal records all of the checks that you write. You must document why each check was written. When it is appropriate, documentation should include a copy of the bill covered by the check. The bill should be marked with the date, check number, and amount paid. If there is no bill, there should be a simple request form agency staff members can use to request checks. This form should include date, amount, payee, reason for payment, name of person requesting the check, and the signature of someone authorized to approve the expenditure. Request forms are used for items such as postage, conference preregistration, mileage reimbursement, et cetera. Your organization should have a procedure whereby all purchases are authorized for payment before the check is written. If this is not possible, it is suggested that the executive director personally initial all bills before signing the check for payment.

For control measures, it is recommended that all operating checking accounts require two signatures for checks. The usual method is to require that both the executive director and one of the corporate officers of the board of directors sign the checks. In the absence of the director, two of the designated officers sign. Relevant documents, such as the original bills or request forms, should be presented with the checks for signature to at least one of the check signers.

At a minimum, an organization should keep a cash receipts journal and a cash disbursements journal to record money received and money spent. If there is a paid staff, a separate payroll journal should be kept that records the amount earned by each employee, the amount withheld for taxes, the amount paid for benefits, and the amount paid to the employee. Sales or fees-earned journals should be kept when this type of income is received regularly by your agency. An organization with a fairly extensive system of billing for fees or publication sales may utilize an accounts receivable journal to keep track of the unpaid bills owed to the agency. Organizations with an accrual-basis accounting system must utilize both an accounts receivable and an accounts payable journal.

The procedures outlined above briefly describe the documenting and recording functions of the bookkeeping system. The summarizing function is performed by the *general ledger*. This is a book with a separate sheet for each category of assets (bank accounts, petty cash, accounts receivable, furniture and equipment), liabilities (accounts payable, loans), income (grants, contracts, fees), and expenses (rent, salaries, supplies, et cetera). At the end of each month, all of the enteries in your journals are totaled and the total for each category of expenses and income is entered onto the appropriate page of the general ledger. Each of these categories is called an *account*. In order to save time and make recordkeeping easier, each account is usually assigned a number. The list of these numbered accounts is referred to as the *chart of accounts*.

FINANCIAL REPORTS: TELLING IT LIKE IT IS

It is from the summary of your financial transactions in the general ledger that you prepare financial reports. These reports take many forms, depending on the organization and its internal needs and the needs of interested persons and organizations outside the agency. No matter how many or how few, how simple or how complex, your financial reports are, there are some general criteria to follow.

Financial Reports Should Be Clear

Any person taking the time to read the document should be able to understand it. Understandable titles, clear descriptions, and a simple format are essential. In-house jargon or codes that would not be understood by someone outside the organization should not be used.

Financial Reports Should Be Concise

Reports should be kept as short as possible so that no one will get lost in detail. There is nothing wrong with presenting two or three short reports rather than one long, detailed one. In some cases, you may wish to give one report or set of reports to the public and keep a more detailed set for your board of directors.

Financial Reports Should Be All-inclusive

Your financial reports should provide a total picture of all the activities of your organization. Reporting on separate programs and funds is important. Even when you keep your books on a cash basis, every effort should be made to include accrued income and expenses in these reports to give a full picture of your financial position. In other words, periodic financial reports should report on income earned or pledged but not yet received and debts owed but not yet paid.

Financial Reports Should Be Comparable

Your reports should have some point for comparison so that the reader will have a basis for arriving at some conclusion about your financial activity over a period of time. This can be in comparison to planned budget figures or to amounts from a corresponding period of time in the previous year.

Financial Reports Should Be Timely

Reports should be issued on a regular (monthly or quarterly) basis, and they should be prepared as soon after the end of the period as possible. Otherwise, they lose their significance and usefulness.

Income and Expense Reports and Balance Sheets

There are two common types of financial reports: income and expense reports and balance sheets. *Income and expense reports* outline income and expense items over a period of time, such as a month, a quarter, or a year. These reports generally include a comparison to budgeted amounts. Such information allows directors, managers, and board members make future spending decisions and helps them plan the budget for future periods. It is highly recommended that these reports be done on a functional basis, showing income and expenses for each program you offer as well as for administrative and fund-raising activities.

Balance sheets and changes in fund balances outline the financial net worth of an organization at a given point in time, usually as of the ending date of a reporting period. The balance sheet shows the total amounts of assets and liabilities and the balances in various funds that the organization has. These balances are generally compared to those at the end of the previous reporting period.

Income and expense reports are generally prepared more often than balance sheets. One common practice is to prepare income and expense reports monthly and income and expense reports and balance sheets quarterly and at the end of the fiscal year.

Fundors and others who review these reports will be looking for indications that your organization is in a strong financial position and that you have established a positive trend in your finances.

Nonprofit organizations may be required by state law to submit an annual financial report, depending on the amount they receive in contributions. It may also be required that this financial report include an official audit report by a certified public accountant (CPA). The state department of commerce can tell you whether or not you are required to submit an annual financial report. An annual audit by a certified public accountant is also required by some fundors and can be a helpful financial review for an organization itself. Your board members or an accounting aid association, if there is one in your city, may be able to help you locate volunteer or low-cost accounting services.

YOU, YOUR BOARD, AND YOUR MONEY

Proper use of your money is safeguarded by a number of financial control practices within your organization. The usual term to refer to these is *internal control*. As you have seen, internal control takes many forms, such as dual-signature checks, approval of expenditures, controlled handling of cash, and so on. In addition, your board of directors plays a very important role in financial control. Final legal responsibility for your organization rests in this body, and, ultimately, final fiscal responsibility rests there, too. Too often, simple steps for guaranteeing the board's input and the ultimate responsibility of the board are forgotten.

The fiscal responsibility of the board of directors should include their formal discussion and approval of your agency's budget (when possible, this should also include the participation of a board committee in the preparation of the budget). The board also should discuss and approve your agency's periodic financial reports. All contracts should be approved by the board, and they should be signed by a board officer and the executive director. A written limit should be placed on the dollar amount and types of expenditures that can be authorized by your executive director without board approval, and all other expenses should be approved by the board, with documentation in the minutes of the board's meeting. A board member should approve all payments for expenses incurred by the executive director.

Regardless of how much board involvement is considered desirable in your organization, you should not minimize the board's financial involvement and responsibility by bypassing the procedures outlined above. Requiring the board's knowledge of financial operations and involvement in financial decision making can ensure effective control of your organization's money.

Bibliography

Accounting and Financial Reporting: A Guide for United Ways and Not-for-Profit Human Service Organizations. United Way of America, 801 N. Fairfax, Alexandria, Va. 22314, 1974. An in-depth but basic guide to accounting for nonprofit agencies. Accounting principles and mechanics are presented in a manner that can be understood by nonaccountants. A good desk reference for bookkeepers and agency directors. (190 pages)

Financial and Accounting Guide for Nonprofit Organizations. By Malvern Gross. Ronald Press, 79 Madison Avenue, New York, N.Y. 10014, 1974. Comprehensive resource text on nonprofit accounting. Detailed presentation of accounting principles, bookkeeping procedures, financial statements, tax reporting, and internal fiscal controls. Directed toward those with some background in accounting and bookkeeping but can be easily read and understood by the patient novice. (540 pages)

Standards of Accounting and Financial Reporting for Voluntary Health and Welfare Organizations. National Health Council, National Assembly of National Voluntary Health and Social Welfare Organizations, and United Way of America, New York. Revised 1974. Explains standards for uniform financial reporting by nonprofit organizations. Directed toward those already familiar with accounting principles. (130 pages)

Up Your Accountability. By Paul Bennett, Taft Products, 1000 Vermont Ave. N.W., Washington, D.C. 20005, 1973. A basic introduction to accounting concepts, bookkeeping, budgeting, and financial reporting. Especially useful for managers of small, nonprofit agencies who have had little or no experience in these areas. Discusses use of accounting reports in making management and program decisions. (66 pages)

Where Do All the $$$ Go? By Gerald Bowe. New Hampshire Charitable Fund, 1 South Street, Concord, N.H., 1975. Very basic introduction to accounting, bookkeeping, and internal controls for nonprofit organizations. (39 pages)

You Don't Know What You Got Until You Lose It. By T. Miller and G. Orser. The Support Center, 1822 Massachusetts Avenue N.W., Washington, D.C. 20036, 1975. Explains what accounting includes and why it is important for nonprofit groups. Very elementary guide to money management by small community groups. (30 pages)

Staff: Building a Team

To a large extent, the identity of your program in the community and with your clients is determined by your staff. The community looks at your staff and sees your agency. A good program plan, a healthy budget, and a committed board cannot carry the ball without a qualified and motivated staff. Personnel issues for the new program include determining staffing needs, developing job descriptions, recruiting the staff, and developing personnel policies.

WHAT KIND OF STAFF DO YOU NEED?

It is important to take the time and energy to consider carefully the staffing needs of your organization. It is more useful to work from tasks to people in outlining your staff, rather than first arbitrarily naming positions and then assigning tasks. For instance, the program plan developed for your organization should specify in writing the goals and objectives of your program and the tasks necessary to reach these objectives. This outline of tasks can be used to determine the staffing pattern required to carry out the planned program.

1. The skills demanded for each task should be determined. The tasks or functions should be clustered by skill areas, such as administration, clerical support, counseling, education, lobbying, community organization, and so on.
2. Next, determine the length of time required to complete each task or function. How often must this function be carried out? Daily, weekly, monthly, annually? How much time will it require?

105

3. Based on these skill groupings and time estimates, you then develop a list of the staff positions necessary to complete your planned tasks. For each position, the task assignments to be completed should be listed.

4. Consider the various staffing patterns available to your organization. There are many options available to organizations besides having full-time paid staff positions. Alternatives can include part-time paid positions, temporary paid staff, paid consultants, volunteers, college interns, and high school students. Creative use of staffing options can trim your budget and provide an energetic and skilled work force that might otherwise be unavailable to community programs. Play around with various combinations of these options to determine which is most workable for your organization. The result should be a list of staff positions and task assignments, with specifications as to the type of employee (full- or part-time, permanent or temporary, paid or voluntary, et cetera) needed to fill each position.

5. Next, determine the salary ranges for each of the paid positions. By contacting other nonprofit agencies with similar staff positions you can find out what salaries they are paying. Salary ranges ($12,000–$15,000 instead of $13,500) allow you to use some discretion when hiring a staff so that you can pay them according to the amount of education and experience they have.

6. Review your list of positions to determine whether such a staffing pattern would realistically allow for completion of the activities outlined in the program plan. Is the staffing pattern realistic in terms of the projected budget? Can you attract persons who have the needed skills with the proposed salaries? At this point, it may be necessary to revise the program plan to meet staff and budget limitations, to expand the budget to allow for a staff adequate to carry out the program plan, or to readjust the staffing pattern to provide the skills you need without depending on a large and costly staff of full-time paid employees.

7. After completing the staff list, develop an organizational chart clarifying the decision-making process and the chain of command within your organization. The chart graphically diagrams supervisory relationships among the staff and outlines proposed reporting and communicating patterns. This diagram allows you to picture where in the organization each position fits. It also helps you determine the level of responsibility of the staff members and the supervisory and administrative skills required in each position. It also allows you to see how the staff members will work together as a team.

ORGANIZATIONAL CHART MODELS

There are a range of models that an organization can follow. On one end of the continuum is a loosley structured team, or whole group, approach in which each member has an equal role and there is no one director. At the other end is the traditional hierarchical structure under a director with broad powers. There are other models that combine features of these two approaches. A fledgling organization can choose one organizational structure and then refine it or change to another model as the organization develops and grows.

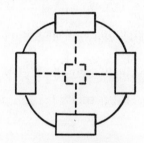

Whole Group Model

Whole Group Model

Especially in small agencies, the whole group can operate as a team. Emphasis is on group decision making. The organization may not have a central administrator or coordinator.

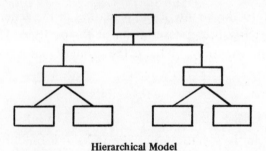

Hierarchical Model

Hierarchical Model

This traditional organizational structure emphasizes the one-to-one supervisor/supervisee relationship. Decisions are generally made by the supervisor with input and feedback from those supervised.

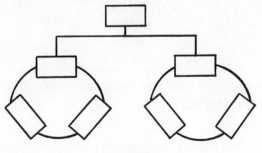

Team Model

Team Model

In larger agencies, the staff can be broken into subgroups, often by program. Each team functions similarly to that in the whole group model. The administrator coordinates the various teams.

Combination

An agency may choose to combine features of these three organizational models to allow both group interaction and individual feedback and appraisal.

JOB DESCRIPTIONS: PUTTING IT ALL ON PAPER

Job descriptions specifically define staff positions, outlining the major responsibilities of each position, its major task and function, and the background necessary to fulfill the responsibility the job entails. Job descriptions should be developed for each staff position, including volunteer and intern positions. Developing job descriptions helps the organization in several ways.

1.   It forces you to explain each position in objective, measurable terms.
2.   It provides a clear, standard description of staff positions for potential applicants.
3.   It serves as a basis for developing screening and selection processes for applicants.
4.   It provides guidelines for job performance and employee evaluation.

Although there are a variety of useful formats for job descriptions, most include three basic parts.

Primary Responsibilities

Generally, this is a one- to three-sentence explanation of the general areas of responsibility and a fairly broad description of the position. The explanation should answer this question: "What is the primary reason this position exists?"

Specific Functions

This section outlines in fairly specific terms the tasks and functions to be performed. One useful format lists each major responsibility as a distinct, one-sentence statement and then outlines the major corresponding tasks for each. The tasks outlined under each single responsibility area are a response to this question: "What would I actually have to do to fulfill this responsibility?"

Education and Experience Requirements

After you know what the person is responsible for and what major tasks the position includes, the next question is what a person *must* know, or what skills and abilities he or she *must* have in order to do those tasks. You should keep asking this question: "If the applicants don't have this knowledge or skill, might they still be able to do the job?"

Sample Job Description Format

Job Title: Youth Counselor

Reports to: Director

Supervises: Counseling Intern

Primary Responsibilities:

Providing individual and group treatment for youths in the program.
Developing individual treatment plans for youths in caseload.

Specific Activities (for each activity area, estimate percentage of time spent):

A. Provide individual counseling for six to eight youths at least once a week, developing treatment plan with the youths, setting up monthly behavioral contracts with them, and assessing their needs.   30%

B. Facilitate daily group sessions with youths.   30%

C. Maintain relationships with families, schools, and court workers of youths and with related community agencies.   20%

D. Facilitate family sessions for those who request it.   10%

E. Develop volunteer service placements for young clients.   5%

F. Serve as member of team of program counseling staff, attend staff meetings, supervise counseling intern.   5%

Requirements:

Skills and knowledge—Demonstrated knowledge of group and individual counseling skills, a working knowledge of community youth resources, ability to work with youths and their families, behavior planning skills.

Education—Training in individual, group, and family counseling.

Experience—At least three years experience in youth work.

Desired skills, education, experience:

B.A. degree in psychology, sociology, or related field.
Skill in planning and implementing recreational activities.
Awareness of alternative educational systems, court services, drugs and their effects, symptoms of learning disabilities.
Experience in youth-outreach work.

Sample Job Description Format

Job Title:

Reports to:

Supervises:

Primary Responsibilities:

Special Activities (for each activity area, estimate percentage of time spent):

Requirements:

   Skills and knowledge—

   Education—

   Experience—

Desired skills, education, experience:

Requiring more extensive education or experience than is essential for the position can lead to potential injustices. It is important to state job requirements in terms of the specific skills needed rather than in terms of related skills or background. If you keep your statements in terms of "knowledge of," "skill in," or "ability to," you should avoid most of the pitfalls.

For example, employers may make the mistake of restricting a job to males instead of listing a job requirement as "must be able to lift 100-pound loads from floor to truck bed." Or a chemical dependency treatment program might unfairly require that all counselor applicants "must have been chemically dependent" instead of requiring "detailed knowledge of the effects of chemical dependency on family dynamics and adolescent development."

Other knowledge and experience that would be helpful in the position can be listed as "desired" rather than "required." This additional information can help applicants understand more about the job, but care should be taken to ensure that the position is not restricted to those who have skills and knowledge listed only as "desired."

Once the necessary positions have been identified and the preliminary job descriptions written, you can begin making decisions about how to advertise, what procedures to use in screening résumés and applications, how you are going to select your final candidate(s), whom you want involved in each of these steps, and when the steps should be taken.

HELP WANTED: ADVERTISING FOR STAFF

The best way to attract qualified staff people is to use as many advertising media as possible. The most commonly used resources are local newspapers, especially the Sunday editions, which reach masses of people. Place your ad, not only in major city newspapers, but also use community, independent, and weekly papers, which have more selected audiences. It is also useful to send your job notices to special interest publications in your field, professional newsletters and journals, related agencies, and placement offices at colleges and universities. If you have a local volunteer placement bureau, you can advertise there for volunteers. You could find interns through college and university departments.

Employment ads should include the job's title, a brief description of the job's responsibilities and functions, a list of the required skills and background, the salary range, the employing agency and its address, the materials required for application, and the deadline for submitting those materials.

This information can be summarized from the basic job description you compiled during the planning stages.

By requiring written résumés or applications, you eliminate the necessity of prescreening applicants in person and over the phone. Personal prescreening can discriminate against those who do not talk to you in person, so it is important to set up consistent prescreening policies. However, by depending solely on written résumés for prescreening applicants, you may discriminate against qualified applicants who simply have not presented themselves well on paper. If you choose written résumés as the method for prescreening applicants (most hiring through social service agencies is done this way), be sure to examine all the résumés carefully, looking for the basic skills you require.

REVIEWING RÉSUMÉS

A simple but fair procedure must be developed for reviewing résumés and judging each applicant's potential for doing the job. This process is necessarily subjective, but the aim is to be as objective as possible. You must be able to get beyond simply saying, "I think I like this person better than that person," and be able to justify that preference based on your actual hiring criteria.

One review method is based on a two-step process: (1) selecting those who indicate that they have the minimum skills required for the job and (2) judging the skill levels of those with at least minimal skills. A written rating scale can be developed for reviewing résumés during these two steps. The knowledge, skills, and experience outlined in the job description are used as criteria for the résumé review tool.

Skill rating based on résumés is not an exact, perfectly reliable science. It is simply an effort to be more precise than depending on totally subjective, off-the-cuff judgments. Keep this shortcoming in mind when designing and using a résumé review tool. Your rating scale should be defined in simple, clear terms so that all involved in the review process have a common understanding of the criteria. The skills and knowledge you require should be translated into measurable terms, when possible.

Each item can be assigned a rating scale, either a two-step (have/do not have minimum capacity) or a three- to five-level scale based on the applicant's number of years' experience, level of responsibility, typing speed, et cetera. Each item should indicate the minimum level of skill or experience acceptable. If applicants do not indicate at least minimal skills in all items, they would not be considered further, unless you later judge a particular requirement to be unfair or unreasonable.

When using the scale, you should not be so restrictive as to eliminate applicants unfairly because they do not have exactly the right kind of experience; people can learn skills through many types of experience, and their capabilities may not be represented on paper exactly as you expect them to be.

It is best when each résumé is reviewed by two to four people. This decreases the influence of personal biases or variant interpretations of the résumés. Your résumé review committee can be composed of appropriate staff members, board members, client representatives, and professionals from related programs or funding sources, according to your needs.

During the initial review step, you should reject only those applicants whom two or more people agree are unqualified. The next step is to judge the quality and quantity of the skills of those applicants who pass the initial review. Again, at least two and preferably three or four people should complete ratings on these applicants. The results of these ratings can be combined during the final screening. As a result of this step, you will develop a small pool of applicants to interview (perhaps five to ten but an exact number should not be set ahead of time).

Before interviewing the final applicants, jot down notes on areas in which you need more specific information, based on their résumés. These can be used to formulate questions for the interview.

INTERVIEWING

In most situations, you can judge the basic skills of applicants through their résumés, but a further step is needed to choose among those who seem to have the ability to do the job. The interview can elicit much more information than it is possible to get in résumés. It gives both the employer and the applicant a chance to ask questions that have developed during earlier stages of the hiring process. However, the flexibility and subjectivity of interviewing make it a double-edged tool. It has the potential of supplying crucial information for decisions, but it also has equal potential for being unfair.

Standardized interviews can be designed to allow you to treat applicants equally and to be able to compare different people. If you do not have parallel information, comparison will be very difficult. Interviews for each applicant can be structured so that they closely resemble each other in content and format. Write down the questions you wish to have answered, ask them of all applicants, use the same interviewers, and develop a means of noting answers and rating them.

Loosely structured interviews rely on questions tailored to each individual applicant. This allows you to round out the information contained in their résumés. It is often helpful to hear applicants explain their experience and skills. This also allows you to determine more specifically the strengths and weaknesses of each applicant and to draw more individual images of each person you interview.

Interviews can be designed to balance standardization with flexibility. Several open-ended questions can be developed that are appropriate for all applicants and allow you to compare responses. Other questions can be developed specifically for each person to be interviewed.

At the beginning of each interview, reiterate the basic job responsibilities, hours, and salary range, explain the hiring process, and answer any specific questions about the job. The interview questions should be open ended. Again, it is best to have two to four people participate as interviewers and to use a combination of their judgments as the basis of the selection.

Another selection tool that can be used is performance testing. Applicants can be asked to spend some time working in one of the programs or to take part in a simulated client session. Copies of the applicant's previous written projects can be reviewed. Clerical applicants can be asked to take a typing test and write a business letter.

You may wish to narrow the choice down to two or three candidates after the first interview and then interview these final candidates a second time. During the second interview, you may wish to involve other staff members who will be working with this person. Since you have already discussed the quality of these candidates, the second interview can focus on related values and attitudes, work style, and preferences regarding management and supervision.

HIRING

After the candidates have been interviewed, but before you make your final selection, contact two to four persons listed as references by the candidates. The most thorough procedure is to ask for written references and to confirm these with a phone call, but sometimes only one or the other form of contact is used. Ask the references to confirm the reliability of the individuals and the quality of their past work. Remember that former supervisors may have biases or personality differences with the candidates, so try to disallow attitudes that may have little to do with the person's capacity to perform well in your agency. Nevertheless, contacting references is still the best way to determine whether the applicants have presented themselves accurately on paper and in person.

When the final selection has been made, the individual should be formally offered the job. Usually, the offer is made by phone and confirmed by letter. The letter of hiring should include a brief summary of the job's responsibilities, the starting salary and fringe benefits provided, an explanation of probationary period (if any), the beginning date of work, the number of work hours expected of part-time employee (if appropriate), any special agreements or arrangements between the agency and the new employee, the signature of the executive director, and a copy of the personnel policies.

As soon as a candidate has accepted the position, all those who applied for the job should be notified as quickly as possible.

FAIR EMPLOYMENT PRACTICES

Caution must be taken to protect the rights of applicants during all phases of hiring. You as a prospective employer must be careful not to place unjust or unsupportable demands on applicants. Be careful to demand knowledge, skills, abilities, and experience that you are confident are necessary to effective job performance. You should be continually asking yourself, "Why do I want this information?" and "Does the answer really have a bearing on the person's ability to do the job?" If you are ever questioned about why you chose certain selection procedures, you will be responsible for proving their validity.

The following areas should never be included as subjects on applications, in résumé reviews, or in interviews: age, race, or sex; marital status, number and age of children, child care arrangements, weekend work capacity (unless part of regular work), credit records, public assistance status, arrest and conviction records, and disabilities (unless they might *directly* interfere with job performance).

If you have problems trying to design fair employment procedures, contact your state department of human rights or the personnel department of larger cities or counties for guidelines.

Carefully document all aspects of your recruitment and hiring practices as a safeguard against allegations of discrimination. The dates and texts of ads and the publications in which the ads were placed should be recorded, and the hiring procedures should be outlined in writing.

PERSONNEL POLICIES

Personnel policies are written guidelines defining the relationship between an agency and its staff. They spell out what the agency expects of the staff, what the staff can expect from the agency, and what the procedures are for resolving work-related conflicts. Well-written policies can promote good communication between your agency and its employees, and they can prevent conflicts arising from misunderstandings.

The board of directors is responsible for the development of written personnel policies. Often, this task is delegated to a personnel committee or to a special ad hoc committee of the board. Ideally, personnel policies should be determined during an early stage of the agency's development. The input of the director of the agency, and of any other staff members who have already been hired, aids the development of workable, satisfactory policies. Ask organizations similar to yours for copies of their policies to use as models. Your own personnel policies, however, should be tailored to fit your own needs and values.

The personnel policies should be formally accepted by the board of directors. They should be reviewed every one or two years and be revised, when necessary, to reflect new organizational needs and capacities. Each employee should be given a copy of the policies.

The following outline can be followed in developing personnel policies.

PERSONNEL POLICY GUIDELINES

Introduction

Briefly describe the process used for writing the policies in an introduction, including the date of approval and the recommended period for reviews of policies.

Employee Definitions

Define *full-time employee, part-time employee* (in terms of numbers of hours worked), *temporary employee, volunteer employee,* and any other classification of employee to be used by your agency. Eligibility for benefits and compensation should be defined.

Hiring Practices

Hiring procedures and policies, including advertisement, screening, selection, and promotion considerations, should be explained. A statement explaining affirmative action and equal employment policies should be included also. (Check to see which federal and state laws apply to your agency because of its size, nature, and funding source.)

Employee Evaluations

Explain employee-evaluation procedures, including probationary periods and periodic performance reviews.

Termination and Grievance Procedures

Practices regarding voluntary termination, involuntary termination, and layoffs, including notification regarding termination, should be specified. Grievance procedures available to employees should be outlined.

Salaries

Agency policy regarding salary schedules, salary reviews, withholding social security benefits, and reimbursement for transportation, overtime, and other expenses should be specified, as should the schedule for paydays.

Benefits

Explain the health and life insurance coverage provided to employees. Any staff development or training benefits should be described, including funds or leaves available to employees for education or training.

Absences, Vacations, and Holidays

Specify paid or unpaid time away from work that is available to employees and rate of accumulation, procedures for arranging time off, eligibility restrictions, and salary policies for each of the following: vacation, sick leave, holidays, personal days, leaves of absence, maternity/paternity leaves, and jury duty.

Hours

The minimum hours of work required per week, the daily office or program hours, and procedures for variances from these should be specified. Will overtime be compensated by additional pay or time off?

Personnel Files

Explain the contents of personnel files, procedures for access, and the procedures for challenging or adding to the materials included in them.

Community Relations: Keeping in Touch

Your doors are open. You have a well-planned program. You have some funding. You have a board of directors and a competent staff. You've got it all together—but something important is still missing. It is the people factor of your program—the reason you put it together in the first place—your "community."

The relations you develop with your community are crucial to the success of your program. Who is your community? It is, first of all, those for whom the program was designed—your clients, or constituency. Depending upon your program, it may also include other agencies, neighborhood residents, community leaders, potential fundors, and others. These various segments of your community are your "publics."

The process of developing effective community relations is also known as public relations. *Public relations* are those functions of an organization concerned with informing the public of its goals, activities, and policies and attempting to create public opinion favorable toward the organization and its mission. Public relations activities include publicity, advertising, newsletters and brochures, membership recruitment, special events, public meetings, and personal interaction of staff and board members with those in the community. Relations with your publics are developed in order to attract clients, members, or participants, to attract financial resources, to convert these resources into programs and services, and to provide these services.

Nonprofit groups, as well as businesses, engage in public, or community, relations. Every organized group is involved in community relations—whether they know it or not and whether they have planned for it or not. And these relations are having an impact on the program—for better or, sometimes, for worse. Unless community relations are developed according to a well-thought-out plan, your efforts in this area will have limited, transitory, and perhaps harmful effects.

119

Developing a plan for effective community relations will help an organization to achieve its program's objectives. The success of a program depends as much on the people outside of the agency as it does on those within. The support of your community—of clients, members, other agencies and professionals, fundors, community residents and leaders—is essential.

Planning effective community relations involves:

1. Defining your community.
2. Determining the objectives of your community relations.
3. Deciding the messages to be conveyed to your community.
4. Selecting the media for communication with your community.
5. Outlining and carrying out your community relations plan.
6. Evaluating the results.

Who should be involved in developing your community relations plan? Both board and staff input is essential for putting together an effective public relations program. It works out best when one person is designated to be ultimately responsible for overseeing the community relations of your organization. If the staff is large enough and has some expertise in this area, a staff member—either paid or volunteer—can perform this role. In many cases, a board member serves as public relations chair, perhaps working with a committee. You may be able to recruit someone with experience in this area to serve as a board member in this role. One option is to have a public relations chair on the board who works closely with one staff person—perhaps the director, assistant director, or information coordinator—to develop and administer community relations plans. In any case, the input of other board and staff members is important; they can bring additional insight and expertise to this planning process, and their support will be needed to carry out your public relations plans.

The following planning guide is supplemented by several forms at the end of this chapter, which are referred to as they are used in the process of planning for community relations.

STEP 1: DEFINE YOUR COMMUNITY (Form A)

The first step in community relations planning is to identify those groups with whom your organization has, or should have, relationships. These groups are your "publics." You probably do not have one broad, homogeneous public; you probably have instead many smaller, identifiable groups. These groups vary according to the nature of the organization. A community theater establishes relationships with theater goers, actors, and others involved in producing a play and fundors interested in the arts. A youth group may want to reach youths, their parents, school officials, other youth agencies in the area.

Some of these groups may be organized—other agencies, service clubs, other special interest associations, political parties, neighborhood associations, and governmental bodies. Some are not organized but are easily identified—members, clients, families of clients, fundors, and certain community leaders. Other groups are larger, unorganized, and less easily identified—senior citizens, music lovers, smokers, potentially delinquent youths, and business people.

In order to identify your publics, ask yourself: to whom will you be providing services? Whom do you want to attract to your program? Will you be referring clients to anyone else? Will you be receiving clients referred from other sources? Who will be providing funding and other support for the program? Are there groups who you will be trying to influence? Who will be trying to influence you? Are there those whose good will you depend on? The answers to these questions should provide you with an outline of the major groups in the community with whom you have or will be establishing relationships.

Each of these major groups, or markets, should then be divided into smaller units, or segments. This segmentation will allow you to examine the differences among each of these groups based on their interests, needs, perceptions, size, et cetera. Your community relations plan should take into account these differences among the segments of your market in order to be more effective in reaching each of these segments. Each may require a different message sent through different media and aimed at different objectives. You may want different things from each of your publics.

It can be helpful to rate the relative importance of each of these segments to your organization. This can help you set priorities for your efforts and avoid spending a lot of time and effort reaching a group who is relatively unimportant to you while you are ignoring another major group. *Importance* can be defined in terms of the extent to which the group can have an impact on your program or the extent to which you feel you can have an impact on them.

STEP 2: DETERMINE THE OBJECTIVES OF YOUR COMMUNITY RELATIONS PLAN (Form D)

What do you want your community relations plan to accomplish? In broad terms, you want your community to support you and to use your resources.

But the objectives of your plan must be more specific. What kinds of community support do you need in order to achieve your program? In many cases, your public relations objectives may parallel your program objectives. As with program objectives, public relations objectives must be specific, realistic, and measurable in terms of numbers of people, dates, money, et cetera. They should be concerned with results rather than process. In addition, they should be agreed upon and written down.

Objectives can be short term, related to a specific community relation effort, or ongoing, aimed at maintaining a certain level of performance. What do you want your public to think or do as a result of your communication with them? This should be something very specific, such as becoming a participant in your program, referring others to your program, providing funding, establishing a service contract with you, supporting your presence in the community, attending a concert, et cetera. You may also want a response that is more difficult to perceive: for example, a change in attitude toward your program or an increase in the level of knowledge about a particular issue. In either case, you should be able to pinpoint the intended response closely enough so that you will later be able to tell whether your communication succeeded.

Examples

1. To attract thirty new participants each month from September through December.
2. To increase by 30 percent the number of clients referred by the community high schools during the following school year.
3. To sell an average of 300 tickets per performance.
4. To develop a service contract with Ramsey County by January 1981.
5. To receive $2,000 in donations by September.
6. To improve the attitude of residents toward the group home in their neighborhood.
7. To maintain theater attendance at the current level for the next season.

STEP 3: DECIDE THE MESSAGES TO BE CONVEYED (Form B)

What information do you wish to convey to each of the publics you have identified? What attitude or impression do you want them to have of your program? What idea do you want to get across? What are you offering to the community? If you have done an adequate job of program planning, this step will be just about complete. You should have already assessed the needs of the community that you will be serving. You should have defined those particular needs that your program will be addressing. And you should have a clear description of the programs and services to be provided.

Use this information to arrive at a description of the program or, in a sense, "product" that you are offering to the community. Briefly outline each service that your organization provides. The need each service meets should be defined. Also, each service's uniqueness should be outlined. What are the characteristics of the service that will appeal to the community you wish to serve? Such features may be related to its availability elsewhere in the community, the background of the staff, the program, its philosophy, its target constituency, its price, and the uniqueness of program. In other words, what should you *stress* about your program when you tell the community about it?

How do each of your publics regard you? What impression do they have of you? This image can be described in terms of expertise, confidence level, comfortability, and accessibility. Are you considered to be competent, trustworthy? Are you considered outsiders in the community? Does your public know what you offer and at what cost and how to get involved in your program?

If you are unsure of your image in the community, develop a feedback mechanism to give you this information. Formal feedback, through polls and surveys, can be difficult to obtain and costly. However, small-scale efforts at surveys can be conducted periodically. Questionnaires completed by current members or participants are relatively easy to develop. However, most of your community feedback will probably be informal. Meetings, interviews, and casual discussions with members of your various publics can tell you much about your program's image when you solicit this input.

In turn, how do you want each of your markets to regard you? What impression of you do you wish them to have? Are there any discrepancies between what people see in you and what you want them to see? How can they be minimized? The results of this exercise are important to consider when you are designing your message to the community. You must take care to establish an identity that you feel truly represents you and design communications that reinforce this image. In some cases, you may have to make some program changes in order to develop a more positive image in the community.

At this point, you should have a good idea of the messages you wish to convey, and you can write your messages out briefly and simply. They will be the basis of your communications with your publics.

Examples

1. Forming block clubs can help prevent crime in your neighborhood.
2. Buying a season theater ticket saves money and time and provides much entertainment.
3. Your financial support will help send fifty handicapped children to camp.
4. We are an effective and qualified program to which you can refer troubled youths.

STEP 4: SELECT THE MEDIA FOR YOUR COMMUNICATION WITH YOUR COMMUNITY (Form C)

The communication media available to you include television and radio spots, newspaper ads and articles, posters, slide shows, brochures, newsletters, booths, speaking engagements, personal meetings, special events, ads in buses, and door-to-door campaigns. The media available offer a range of possibilities and vary in the amount of money and expertise they require. The resources listed in the bibliography for this chapter do a good job of describing the pros and cons of various media. Consider the media carefully and select those you wish to use to reach your audience. (Generally, use more than one type of communication to convey your message.) Certain media may be more effective for reaching a particular audience than others.

Where is your audience located? In other words, where can you reach them? Are they generally at home, in school, at work, in clubs, involved with the courts or other agencies? This information provides a key to choosing the most appropriate medium for reaching your audience.

What else do they do? This question provides supplemental information and is often helpful in choosing your main medium or a secondary channel of communication. What kind of activities do they participate in: watching television, listening to the radio, attending church or other social activities, participating in clubs or cultural activities, going to a doctor? Perhaps you can reach your audience by using channels that they are already using.

When selecting media, ask yourself: Will this medium help us achieve our goals? Will it reach our target audience? Can we do a good job with this medium? Can someone help us use it more effectively? How much will it cost? Can we afford it? Are the projected results worth the cost?

STEP 5: OUTLINE AND CARRY OUT YOUR COMMUNITY RELATIONS ACTIVITIES (Form D)

The next step is to convert your community relations ideas into a workable plan. As a result of the last exercise, you should have considered possible channels of communication, the costs and resources required by each, their potential impact, and any drawbacks they may have. Draw on the resources of your board members to help make the decision regarding the most appropriate media for your purposes. If none of your board members has expertise in this area, chances are they can draw on the skills of others they know or work with.

Once you have made these decisions, outline the specific activities that correspond to each of the community relations objectives you already identified.

Examples

1.   Design and distribute 500 brochures regarding our agency to potential referral sources.
2.   Prepare a press release regarding the organization's stand on proposed legislation to be sent to local daily and community newspapers.
3.   Design a booth to represent the agency at a state conference in March.
4.   Conduct personal meetings with staff at twelve agencies and schools that are potential referral sources.
5.   Develop a radio spot explaining the hotline aimed at youths and place it with youth-oriented stations.

Realistically outline your community relations plan in terms of the resources necessary: people, time, materials, and money. What can your agency afford? These costs should be considered when you plan your budget. Time and money spent on community relations is not a frivolous extra; it can be crucial to the success of your organization.

For each activity, pinpoint the date, at least by month, by which the activity should be complete. Identify the staff member who will complete the activity or take responsibility for its completion. Any needed resources should be identified: equipment, facilities, information, skills outside of your agency. Determine the cost of completing this activity. Such expenses may include production or printing costs, paper, postage, computerized mailing lists, consulting or design fees. You may also wish to determine how much the activity will cost in terms of staff time, converted to a dollar figure, when possible.

The list of resources, skills, and expenses may seem overwhelming initially, but consider all of the resources in your community that can provide help: public relations, advertising, and graphic arts departments of the businesses and corporations that fund you, that your board members work for, or that may be interested in providing such a donation can provide design, production, and printing assistance. Public relations and advertising agencies may be interested in adopting a nonprofit agency for a period as a public service. Professional associations of journalists and other communication professionals may help you locate volunteers. Schools of journalism and/or advertising at local colleges and universities may be interested in helping you. A media resource center for nonprofit agencies may be available, if you are in a large metropolitan area.

STEP 6: EVALUATE YOUR COMMUNITY RELATIONS EFFORTS (Form D)

After you have carried out your planned activities, it is important to determine what you have accomplished. For each activity, determine how you will evaluate its success (form D).

What questions can be asked that, when answered, will tell you whether the community relations objective has been met? You may have to set up an information or recordkeeping system that will allow you to answer these questions.

Examples

1. How many callers heard about you through the radio spot? (You will have to ask them.)
2. How many clients were referred by the agencies you met with? (You will have to record this information.)
3. How many of the local media carried your press release? (Follow up and keep clips of those that were printed.)

If you received outside assistance in designing your communication, you can approach your volunteers or consultants again after the results are in to help you determine what went right or wrong, how future results could be improved, and how to follow up on this communication.

After you have carried out one community relations program and evaluated its effectiveness, you will be able to develop the next phase in your effort to communicate with your public. Community relations must be an ongoing process of listening to the concerns of your identified community, telling them what you have to say about your issue or your program and listening again for their response.

TAKE IT A BIT AT A TIME

To the novice in the field of community relations, the plan just described probably seems overwhelming. Your initial list of the various groups that make up your community and the subgroups within them will probably seem enormous and out of your control. It is! The utility of this planning guide is that it can help you identify potential community relations activities. From the endless agenda of things you could be doing to interact with the various groups in your community, you must choose which are the highest priority, are most feasible, are affordable in terms of time as well as money, and will most likely get results.

Begin with a limited plan and choose a few selected activities that you feel you can do well. When these are completed, review what you have done. How did it go? What could you have done better? What did you do well? Did you get some results? Where do you go from here?

After you have completed one or two well-planned community relations projects, you will have the confidence to go on to more.

THE MEDIA FOR YOUR MESSAGE

MEDIA	PROS	CONS	MOST EFFECTIVE USE
Personal contacts, meetings	Trust more easily established. More control of communication. Immediate feedback possible: give and take with audience. Communication can be lengthy.	Time consuming. Impractical on large-scale basis.	Best used to introduce your program or idea to selected individuals or groups on whom you rely for clients, funding, support, et cetera.
Brochures, fliers (mass mailed)	Go directly to each individual or agency. Relatively inexpensive. Low budget pieces can be effective. Message can be retained over time.	Compete with tons of other mail. Audience may not take time to read all of your message.	Prepare a good mailing list: up-to-date, the right audience. Design for both skim and detail reading. Make it easy to read; carefully consider color, folding, type, content.
Posters, billboards	Potential of reaching wide audience. Easy to deliver. Inexpensive to produce.	Compete with other visual stimuli. People won't stop to read it.	Grab attention and express message briefly. Message should be clear, short, easy to read. Select sites for a purpose.
Newspaper and magazine ads	Reach a reading audience. Longer messages possible. Potential of a wide audience.	Compete with other information in the publication. Repeated ads in larger publications are expensive.	Use attention-getting message plus supplemental information. Give phone number for further reference. Choose publication and circulation area with target audience in mind.
Newsletter announcements and ads	Reach specialized audiences with identified interests. Inexpensive.	Newsletter may cut or rewrite your message. Publication may be late.	Tailor your message to specific audiences. Have flexible format to allow for cuts and rewrites. Allow plenty of time for dated messages.

THE MEDIA FOR YOUR MESSAGE (Continued)

MEDIA	PROS	CONS	MOST EFFECTIVE USE
Radio	Required to present certain amount of public service announcements (PSAs) without charge. Stations have rather clearly defined audiences. A portable media, goes where audience goes.	No visual image; audio must carry message alone. Must rely on announcer's skill to relay message, or submit well-produced tape.	Avoid details or complexity. Take advantage of listeners' imagination to create images. Repetition of brief messages can be more effective. Refer listeners to other source: "see our ad," "look us up in phone book."
Television	Required to present certain amount of public service announcements (PSAs) without charge. Potential for strong audio and visual impact. Potential for reaching wide audience in their homes.	Competes with well-produced, slick ads and programs. PSAs often appear at odd hours. Producing good spot can be expensive; professional assistance necessary. Potential audience may be difficult to define.	Keep your spot simple and low key; don't try to compete with other productions. Keep message clear and brief. Creat a visual image that reinforces your message. Inject humor when appropriate; TV is an entertainment medium.
Slide shows and videotapes	Potential for dramatic portrayal of your program or idea. Audio and visual appeal. Opportunity for longer messages. Portable; can be delivered to any audience. Little competition for attention of audience (depending on viewing situation).	Expensive to produce. Professional assistance and equipment required. Takes time for planning and producing. Equipment needed for ongoing presentations. If not well done, can be disastrous.	Make sure production is done well; get professional assistance. Use as supplement to other public relations efforts. Plan production carefully. Generate appropriate audiences for your show.

Example for Form A

COMMUNITY RELATIONS: DETERMINE WHOM YOU WANT TO REACH

PUBLICS: What are the major groups with whom your agency interacts?	PUBLIC SEGMENTS: What are the smaller subgroups within each of these markets?	RELATIVE IMPORTANCE (1 = High, 5 = Low)
Junior and senior high youths in the community	Those with drug-use problems	1
	Those using drugs with no problems as yet	2
	Those with friends who have drug-use problem	2
	General student population: health, social sciences	3
Parents	Parents of youth identified as problem users	1
	PTA members	4
	Parents who have drug-use problems	2
	Other parents of junior and senior high youths	4
School personnel	Administrators	3
	Counselors	2
	Social workers	2
	Nurses	3
	Teachers of health and social sciences	3
	Other teachers	4
	Librarians	4
Youth agencies	Recreation programs	4
	Treatment programs	3
	Group homes	2
	Court and diversion programs	2
	Hotlines	2
	Counseling agencies	3
	Clinics	2
	Churches	4
Fundors	County	2
	City	3
	Local foundations and corporations	4

Example for Form B

COMMUNITY RELATIONS: DETERMINE YOUR MESSAGE

PUBLICS: Whom do you want to reach?	What is their current ATTITUDE toward you/your service/your issue?	What do you want them to THINK and/or DO?	MESSAGE: What should you TELL them?
Parents of kids who may have drug-use problems.	Concerned about their kids; unsure of how to help. Unable to relate kid's drug use to their own, in many cases. Uncertain, perhaps afraid, about seeking counseling for themselves or their kids.	Feel okay about coming in for counseling. Be aware of our services. Call us about their concern. Reflect on their own drug use.	If you think your kid is misusing drugs, we can help. Call and talk to us, or set up an appointment to come in. Your drug-using behavior may influence your kids.

Example for Form C

COMMUNITY RELATIONS: WHAT MEDIA CAN YOU USE TO REACH YOUR AUDIENCE?

Whom do you want to reach?	Where can they be reached?	What else do they do?	MEDIA: How can you reach them?
Parents of kids who may have drug-use problems.	At home In civic and community groups PTA meetings Churches Doctors' offices Shopping centers	Watch television Listen to the radio Read local papers Attend recreational events	Speakers at meetings of various groups Radio spots Appearance on local television talk show Newspaper article Posters in stores, bowling alleys, doctors' offices, churches, et cetera.

Example for Form D

COMMUNITY RELATIONS: COMMUNITY RELATIONS PLAN

OBJECTIVES	ACTIVITIES	DATES	STAFF	RESOURCES	COSTS	EVALUATION
To increase by 50 percent the number of parents who call or come in for counseling	Conduct twelve speaking engagements for parents groups	September–May	Sharon/coordinator	List of clubs, groups, et cetera Pool of speakers Handouts Brochure about speakers' bureau	Printing: $300 Transportation: $25	How many speaking sessions were conducted? How many attended? What was the feedback from club or group? Were calls from parents increased as a result?

Form A

COMMUNITY RELATIONS: DETERMINE WHOM YOU WANT TO REACH

PUBLICS: What are the major groups with whom your agency interacts?	PUBLIC SEGMENTS: What are the smaller subgroups within each of these markets?	RELATIVE IMPORTANCE (1 = High, 5 = Low)

Form B

COMMUNITY RELATIONS: DETERMINE YOUR MESSAGE

PUBLICS: Whom do you want to reach?	What is their current ATTITUDE toward you/your service/your issue?	What do you want them to THINK and/or DO?	MESSAGE: What should you TELL them?

Form C

COMMUNITY RELATIONS: WHAT MEDIA CAN YOU USE TO REACH YOUR AUDIENCE?

Whom do you want to reach?	Where can they be reached?	What else do they do?	MEDIA: How can you reach them?

Form D

COMMUNITY RELATIONS: COMMUNITY RELATIONS PLAN

OBJECTIVES	ACTIVITIES	DATES	STAFF	RESOURCES	COSTS	EVALUATION

Bibliography

Effective Promotion: A Guide to Low Cost Use of Media for Community Organizations. Do It Now Foundation, P.O. Box 5115, Phoenix, Ariz. 85010, 1977. Discusses the basics of getting your message across through the mass media—newspaper, radio, television. Topics include analyzing local media, conducting a press conference, issuing a press release, and developing public service announcements for radio and television. Helpful for those making basic decisions about the use of media for community education and public relations. (22 pages)

Effective Public Relations for Community Groups. By Howard and Carol Levin. New York: Associated Press, 1969. Discusses how to develop a public relations campaign in nonprofit organizations. Topics include print media, radio, and television; writing for public relations; recruiting members; direct mail fund-raising campaigns; and special events. (192 pages)

How to Do Leaflets, Newsletters and Newspapers. New England Free Press, 60 Union Square, Somerville, Mass. 02143, 1976. Excellent resource for the novice who needs to become an expert (more or less) very quickly. Outlines all the steps in producing written communications. Includes explanation of types of articles, interviews, writing styles and techniques, editing, scheduling a publication, graphic design, layout and pasteup, printing processes and costs. Includes lots of helpful illustrations. (44 pages)

How to Publish Community Information on an Incredibly Tight Budget. Do It Now Foundation, P.O. Box 5115, Phoenix, Ariz. 85010, 1976. A printing primer for beginners interested in producing fliers, posters, brochures, newsletters. Discusses printing processes, layout, paper, ink pasteup, costs, copyrights, mailing. Outlines useful tools of the trade. Provides definitions of printing and graphics terms. (22 pages)

Marketing for Nonprofit Organizations. By Philip Kotler. Englewood Cliffs, N.J.: Prentice-Hall, 1975. Examines in detail all the basic marketing principles, focusing their application on nonprofit organizations. Discusses client-oriented services, marketing research, program design, promotion decisions, and marketing planning. Includes case studies of government and nonprofit agencies. Most of the terminology is related to business and most of the examples are large agencies, but the book is also useful for small organizations. It introduces concepts and strategies that can be adapted for use by any group. Although it is detailed and textbookish, it does not demand any previous background in business or marketing. (435 pages)

Media Directory for Minneapolis-St. Paul. Minneapolis Communications Center, 3010 Fourth Avenue S., Minneapolis, Minn. 55408, 1980. Provides a listing of about 100 Twin Cities-area media—daily and weekly newspapers, neighborhood newspapers, student papers, magazines, radio and television stations—with deadlines, guidelines, and contact names. Also includes information about writing news releases and public service announcements and examples of each. Important resource for those who wish to relay messages through Twin Cities media or for those in other areas who want an example of what a media directory should include. (Many major metropolitan areas have similar directories.) (44 pages)

Nonprofit Management
Bibliography

The following bibliography lists resources that discuss the ongoing management of nonprofit agencies.

Corporate Planning for Nonprofit Organizations. By James Hardy. Learning Resources Corporation, 7594 Eads Avenue, La Jolla, Cal. 92037, 1972. Designed specifically for nonprofit organizations. This large reference book with a loose-leaf format outlines a planning process that is based on management and behavioral science findings. (120 pages)

Effective Leadership in Voluntary Organizations. By Brian O'Connell. New York: Association Press, 1976. Introductory handbook to administrative concerns of voluntary organizations. Topics include membership recruitment, the role of the president, planning, fund raising, staff recruitment and training, balancing staff and volunteers, running meetings, and evaluation results. (202 pages)

The Effective Management of Volunteer Programs. By Marlene Wilson. Volunteer Management Association, 279 S. Cedar Brook Road, Boulder, Colo. 80302, 1976. Practical handbook for those who manage programs staffed to any extent by volunteers. Chapters cover motivation, organizational climate, planning and evaluation, designing jobs and recruiting to fill them, interviewing and placing volunteers, and training. (197 pages)

Grantsmanship Center News. Grantsmanship Center, 1015 W. Olympic Boulevard, Los Angeles, Cal. 90015. Subscriptions: $15 (bimonthly, per year). Often covers areas of management such as accounting, public relations, and personnel issues, although the major focus of this journal is fund raising.

How to Make Meetings Work: The New Interaction Method. By Michael Doyle and David Straus. San Francisco: Wyden Books, 1976. Guide to author's interaction method for making meetings productive and democratic. Covers such topics as being a good facilitator, recorder, or group member; choosing meeting rooms; making a presentation; and developing agendas for meetings. Includes checklist for rating aspects of meetings. (301 pages)

Making Change: A Guide to Becoming Effective. By Eileen Guthrie and Sam Miller. Interpersonal Communication Programs, 300 Clifton, Minneapolis, Minn. 55403, 1978. Deals with the personal experience of being an effective member of a group—an organization, a staff, or a board of directors. Chapters discuss community change, the "process politician," personal needs of group members, group effectiveness, action planning, successful meetings, and conflict resolution. (199 pages)

Management Evaluation Manual. United Way of Greater St. Louis, St. Louis, Mo., 1977. A lengthy checklist that is useful for measuring an agency's effectiveness in four management areas: nonprofit agency criteria, planning, personnel practices, and fiscal control. (60 pages)

Management: Tasks, Responsibilities, Practices. By Peter Drucker. New York, N.Y.: Harper and Row, 1973. An in-depth guide to business and service agency management. This heavyweight text deals with techniques of effective management and the role of the manager. Drucker is considered a leader in the human relations management field. (818 pages)

Managing Human Services. International City Management Associations, 1140 Connecticut Avenue N.W., Washington, D.C. 20036, 1977. A basic text and reference for the management of social services by local units of government. Over thirty contributing authors examine the role of the city and county in social services, planning and needs assessment, coordination with intergovernmental and private agencies, administrative structures, financial control, and program evaluation. Case studies in a variety of fields are presented. (580 pages)

Managing Nonprofit Organizations. By Diane Borst and Patrick Montana. New York: AMACOM (a division of the American Management Association), 1977. Collection of thirty papers written by experts in the nonprofit sector demonstrating how the systems approach, management by objectives, program budgeting, and business management styles are currently being applied and adapted to all kinds of nonprofit organizations. Includes discussion of basic elements of the management process: planning, organizing, and fiscal control. (336 pages)

MBO for Nonprofit Organization. By Dale McConkey. AMACOM, 135 W. 50th, New York, N.Y. 10020, 1975. Introduces the concept of management by objectives and describes its application to nonprofit organizations. Discusses establishment of objectives, implementing MBO, the role of managers, and performance evaluation. Several case studies are included. (208 pages)

Presenting Performances: A Handbook for Sponsors. By Thomas Wolf. New England Foundation for the Arts, 8 Francis Avenue, Cambridge, Mass. 02138, 1977. Excellent handbook for small, largely volunteer performing arts organizations. Covers incorporation, trustees, financial management, contracts, dealing with performers, promotion, fund raising, and technical aspects of making a performance happen. Lively writing and creative illustrations turn this book into a performance of its own. (160 pages)

Self-evaluation Handbook for Voluntary Action Organizations. National Center for Voluntary Action, 1214 16th Street N.W., Washington, D.C. 20036, 1977. An elementary guide to self-evaluation by agencies. The handbook defines evaluation, outlines models for self-evaluation, and discusses the relationship between planning and evaluation, data collection, and standards of performance. A fifty-five item self-evaluation checklist is included. (44 pages)

Social Work Administration. By Harleigh Trecker. New York: Association Press, 1971. Basic text in administration of social service agencies. Chapters cover the role of administrators, agency-community relations, staff roles, board functions, decision making, policy determination, financial management, agency evaluation, and management principles. (275 pages)

Index

Index

145

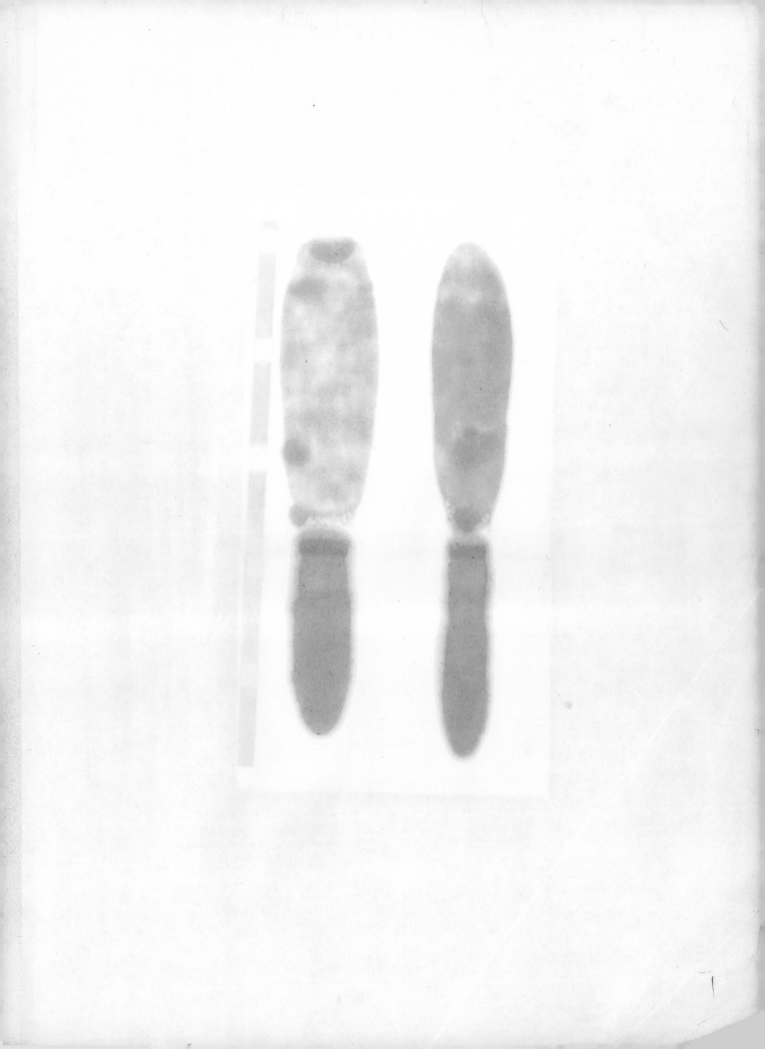